Self-Confidence Made Simple

French Women share their Self-esteem Secrets

By Dr Margaretha de Klerk (nom de plume: Margaretha Montagu)

MargarethaMontagu.com

EquineGuidedGrowth.com

MargarethaMontagu@gmail.com

Previously published as French Women's Confidence Secrets

by SemperEquus

Invitation

Join me on a virtual visit to one of the most unspoilt parts of south-west France, where you can meet our horses and lose yourself in the gorgeous pictures of the meadows, mountains, lakes, orchards, vineyards, lost-in-time villages, decadently delicious food and outstanding wines of this region while you listen to some of the most beautiful French chansons ever written. It will only take 10 magical minutes to recharge your batteries and come back bursting with supreme self-confidence.

All you have to do is to fill in your e-mail address below and subscribe to my blog where you will find empowering tips, motivating quotes, inspiring articles and lots of how-to blog posts. Subscribers receive a copy of my 10 Steps to Instant Self-Confidence guide - straight from the horse's mouth!

Reading my blog will enable you to

- Discover what is wrong with the south of France
- Read more about mindfulness meditation and find your own way to a better practice
- Use mindfulness and meditation to free yourself from your immobilising fear and deal with stress more effectively
- Get access to my equine-guided mindfulness meditation online course
- Find out more about equine-assisted personal development and how to connect with horses
- and learn how to make a decadently-delicious Mousse au Chocolat Noir.

Go to my website at EquineGuidedGrowth.com or click here and fill in your e-mail address to receive news of my workshops here in the south of France with details of last-minute discounts and early bird special offers, available only to my mailing list subscribers. Your adventure starts right away and you will shortly be off to the south of France! Your e-mail address is 100% safe and you can unsubscribe from my blog at any time.

Copyright © by Margaretha de Klerk aka Margaretha Montagu

Contents

Invitation

Contents

Dedication

Foreword

Introduction

About the Author

French women are confident:

- Because they know how to look after themselves - Chapter 1 Sumptuous Self-Care
- Because they know exactly who they are - Chapter 2 Choosing and Changing Your Identity
- Because they know how to keep their lives in balance - Chapter 3 Balancing Act
- Because they have extensive support systems - Chapter 4 Rock-Solid Support Systems
- Because they never forget how much they have to be grateful for - Chapter 5 Gratitude and Generosity
- Because they know how to deal with stress and make it work for them - Chapter 6 Stress Management
- Because they do not allow resentment to erode their confidence - Chapter 7 Forgiveness
- Because they know how to age exactly the way they want to - Chapter 8 Confronting Age
- Because they are pro-active - Chapter 9 Implementation of the French Approach

Conclusion

Bibliography

Links in the text to:

- Self-care Quiz

- Self-Confidence Quiz
- Self-Criticism Quiz
- Stress Quiz
- Vision Board Guide
- Creative Visualisation Guide

Dedication

To the 5 most influential women in my life: my mother, my stepmother, my aunt Angela, my godmother Salomie, my second mother Riet and my mother-in-law Anne.

Special mention: my soul-mare Belle

I am blessed to have several strong women as role models and mentors in my life. During my childhood and early adulthood, my mother encouraged me to be become the best version of myself that I possibly could. Thanks to her encouragement, I chose to go to medical school at a time when only a hundred students were accepted annually at the university of my choice. Only twenty of these students were women. Hundreds of hopefuls applied every year. My mother and father encouraged me, and with their support, I qualified as a doctor six years (and a lot of very hard work) later. Sadly, my mother died of breast cancer during my twenties.

My godmother, my mother's sister Salomie, helped me to stay balanced. When my mother encouraged me to reach for the stars, my aunt Salomie reminded me to stop from time to time and smell the flowers. She taught me the value of looking at life from a different perspective. She taught me not to take myself, or anyone else for that matter, too seriously.

My mother's death, after four years of suffering, was hard to cope with. It would have been much worse had it not been for the constant presence of my aunt Angela, one of my father's sisters. She and her husband owned a vineyard in Stellenbosch in South-Africa. Here I spent many a happy summer as a child learning everything I needed to know about the confidence and courage of the women of my father's family.

My father remarried after my mother died. This could have been a difficult time, was it not for the sensitivity of my stepmother. She taught me what it means to be a good listener. Whenever I have a problem, I discuss it with her. I know that I will get a non-judgemental reception and advice only if I ask for it.

More recently, I have had to undergo several painful eye operations, as the surgeons tried to preserve my sight. I would never have made it through to the other side if it had not been for my dearest friend and second mother Riet. Without her unfailing support and relentless encouragement, I would have given up a long time ago.

I have known my mother-in-law, Anne, for nearly ten years now. In this time, she has enriched my life in more ways than I can count. Anne taught me a lot about gratitude and generosity. She also taught be a fair bit about nurturing friendships.

If would be neglectful if I didn't mention my Friesian mare, Belle de la Babinière. She has been my constant companion, confidante, confidence-booster and supporter for the last ten years. I am infinitely grateful to have her in my life. I am grateful for everything she taught me about myself and about how to help others. Unshakably confident herself, she has taught countless participants in my equine-assisted personal empowerment Connect with Horses workshops how to overcome their fears and confidently live purposeful and fulfilling lives.

A huge and heartfelt thank you to each and every one of you, dearest friends.

"At times, our own light goes out and is rekindled by a spark from another person. Each of us has cause to think with deep gratitude of those who have lighted the flame within us."

Albert Schweitzer

Foreword

Dear Reader,

Thank you so much for buying this book. I hope that you will not only enjoy reading it, but that you will also find much between these pages that will help you become the unwaveringly self-confident, serenely sophisticated and perfectly poised woman that you deserve to be. Regretfully, not that many of us grew up in an environment that nurtured our budding self-confidence, so rather a lot of us have to work at it, sometimes on a daily basis. All is not lost! It is perfectly possible to increase your self-confidence no matter how many times you fell down and had to struggled to get up again. In this book I introduce you to the strategies that have worked for me and for the participants in the personal empowerment workshops that I host here in the south of France.

I wrote this book because I have seen what even a small increase in self-confidence can help women achieve. It is my dearest wish that this book will enable you to discover how smart you are and what you can achieve if you are willing to believe in yourself. I wish I could say that I now am supremely self-confident myself and that I now know everything there is to know about confidence building. Far from it, I am afraid. I learn more with every workshop, so I do update this book as frequently as I can and of course I write blog posts, post on Facebook, LinkedIn and Twitter whenever I discover something that might be of use to my followers.

I am hoping that this book will empower you to

- make quick decisions in difficult situations based on what is really important to you
- accept yourself and appreciate your unique talents and abilities
- believe in yourself so that you can make the changes you want to make in your life
- deal with stress before it damages your physical or mental health
- care for yourself physically, mentally and spiritually

- build strong long-lasting relationships
- create a solid and reliable support network so that you can
- ask for help before you feel totally overwhelmed
- set firm boundaries and say NO without feeling guilty or needing to explain
- focus on what you can learn from an experience rather on what went wrong
- realise that whatever age you are at is the best age for you to be
- stop criticising yourself and
- celebrate your success without needing to apologise for being brilliant

If it doesn't then you may need a bit more help putting these principles into practice. To do so, I recommend that you find yourself a role model, or even better, a mentor, someone with whom you can talk things through. Or you can come to one of my workshops and teach me a few more things I can use to help others. This book is about the conviction that many women hold that French women are more confident than other women. I am not sure if this is true. Parisian women, maybe, maybe not. I have included the stories of more than 10 French woman in this book, so you can judge for yourself.

One thing most French women know is that mentors and role models can give guidance and direction to their lives at times when it feels as if they have lost their way. Not just when they are teenagers or young adults, but every day of their lives, for as long as they live. We need role models, especially as we get older, in our 40s, 50s, 60s, 70s and onward now more than ever, as our conception of what is and what isn't possible as we age is changing. Your role model may be someone you know personally, but it doesn't have to be. It should be someone you admire, who has walked a similar path to the one you find yourself on now and who has succeeded in coping with the challenges that your chosen path presents. Knowing that someone has coped with and solved problems similar to yours is a great confidence-booster. Their situation does not absolutely need to be exactly the same as yours. You will find inspiration and motivation to succeed by choosing any female role model who has conquered her demons, despite the odds.

I will discuss role models and mentors again in one of the chapters that follow, but I have decided bring it up here too, in the foreword to this book, because I want to mention a woman here who has taught me an enormous amount about self-confidence. She is not French, although she has lived for nearly the last two decades here in France, so she has a fairly good idea what being French is all about.

Have you ever noticed how it is only when you nearly lose someone that you realise how important that person is to you? We all know full well how important it is to appreciate the people we love, we just do not always get around to doing so, on a regular basis. I lost two of my best friends in 2018, my horse Aurileo d'Alegria and our beautiful black Newfoundland x Belgian Sheppard Melchi'ore and I nearly lost someone I have come to depend on - my mentor, mother-in-lieu and role model - all in one.

She taught me how infinitely precious the example of a successful role model and supportive mentor can be. Research shows that our confidence increases when we find out that other women have succeeded in reaching similar objectives as the ones we have set ourselves. We realise that it is possible to make our dreams come true, no matter how insurmountable the obstructions we face may seem. Even though we can be inspired by any successful woman, modelling ourselves on women who are similar to ourselves, has the greatest impact on our self-confidence. We end up thinking, "if she can do it, then so can I!" I have kept going, by thinking this many times, over the last 2 or 3 years.

Modelling yourself on a successful example is one of the most helpful principles of Neuro-Linguistic-Programming. I recommend that you identify at least one role model now, at the beginning of this book, more as you go along. If you want to start your own business, your role model may be a successful businesswoman (older or younger!) working in the same field as you. Same goes for artists, students, parents, teachers, carers, actors, athletes, musicians…no matter what you are trying to achieve, having a suitable role model will make it easier. Open your favourite browser and do a search. If you are a businesswoman, you may try "successful women entrepreneurs," for example. I did a search for "successful women writers" and found loads of entries, including a very good article about "The 10 most powerful women authors." The introductory paragraph hit me full-frontal in the gut: "The women selected for this list are powerful because of their ability to influence us through their words and ideas. Collectively, these women hold readers captivated with stories of fantastical worlds, suspense and drama, insights into the complexities of minority experiences and cultures, and fresh takes on societal issues and expectations…not to mention, book sales of up to 800M copies sold and a wealth of prestigious awards and recognition including Nobel and Pulitzer Prizes." Yes! This is the sort of writer I want to be! Some of the women mentioned I already admire and use as role models: Simone de Beauvoir, Margaret Atwood, Isabelle Allende, Maya Angelou… To identify more role models, I do a search to find out more about the other writers mentioned, to read about their lives and the obstacles they had to overcome to be the successful authors they are today. Very difficult not to be inspired. Now it is your turn. Go and do a search and then come back here because I want to make a few more hopefully helpful suggestions.

When you have identified your ideal role model(s), follow the ones who inspire you to be the person you are striving to become, on social media. Many successful women have Twitter, Facebook, Instagram and YouTube accounts…some even have blogs. You can read books, articles, blog posts etc about what these women have achieved but the best way to learn from them is still directly from the horse's mouth. We live in a digital age, where we have access to other people's daily thoughts, we might as well use our opportunities.

Do take care, though, not to fall into the intimidation-trap. Look up to your role model, by all means, but try not to be blinded by their achievements. Don't think, "I'll never be able to achieve what she has achieved!" Remember, like you, she had to start at the bottom. Remember that you are a very special person in your own right and you have your own talents, experience and skills. You might have to walk a path parallel to hers and might not be able to follow in her exact footsteps. Learn from your role models, make their skills your own but be your own woman.

So, choose your role model carefully. It needs to be someone you can relate to, who found themselves in the same situation initially and who had to face the same challenges as you do. One of the most important criteria in choosing a role model is that it should be someone who has the same values as you have and who makes decisions in line with her values. Choosing someone you cannot relate to, who do not hold the same values dear as you do, can result in feelings of insecurity, inadequacy, envy and a dramatic drop in self-confidence. And if your role model should disappoint you, move on, find another. No one is perfect, we all make mistakes.

Although a role model can have a very positive influence, a mentor can be even more effective. The difference between a role model and a mentor as far as I can make out is all about access. A role model could be someone you admire from afar, whereas a mentor is someone you can interact with on a regular basis.

Find yourself a mentor and use this book to become a woman who knows exactly who she is, who takes excellent care of herself, who leads a balanced, purposeful and fulfilling life, who has a solid support network, who can laugh at herself, who knows she has a lot to be grateful for, who knows how to forgive, who competently handles stress, who knows how to say NO without apologising. You too can have the effortless elegance, the enchanting independence, the irresistible charm and the unshakable self-confidence that French women often seem to have.

Btw, all the downloads mentioned in the e-book version of this book are free and that the book contains NO affiliate links. Also, I would also hugely appreciate it if you would let me know if you find spelling mistakes in the text. English is not my first language, so despite my best intentions, mistakes do slip in.

All the very best from the south of France

Margaretha

'I think the best role models for women are people who are fruitfully and confidently themselves, who bring light into the world.' Meryl Streep

(definitely one of my role models)

Une confiance imperturbable en soi est le premier élément de succès.

Diane de Beausacq ; La mode et la Parisienne (1867)

Introduction

I opened the car door and carefully placed my borrowed Louboutins on the tarmac. Tottering over to the sliding doors felt like walking on soft, sticky toffee. The resemblance stopped there. There was no smell of melting sweetness, the city air was thick with pollution. My thin summer dress was sticking to my back. That summer, one heat wave relentlessly succeeded another in the south of France. The south of France is not the paradise it is made out to be. If you want to find out what is wrong with the south of France, visit my blog at EquineGuidedGrowth.com and search for "What is wrong with...." The only reason I left the sanctuary of my ancient farmhouse to come into the city during siesta time was to support my French friend Anais. Anais was taking part in a fashion show. I wished I could leave the Louboutins right there in the middle of the road. I am a horsewoman. As a rule, I am much more comfortable in riding boots. Not so my super-stylish friend Anais. Anais is as chic as she has been when we were teenagers. No, correction. She is now sleeker and more stylish than ever before. No wonder the designer chose her as one of his catwalk models. He designs exclusively for women over forty. Anais, at any age, is so elegant that she can make the drabbest dress look classy.

I made it to the seat in the front row that Anais had reserved for me. I had attended three faultless rehearsals here during the last two weeks. I was confident that today too would be a huge success. So it was, at least for the first four times that Anais walked down the catwalk. Her neat posture and natural poise displayed the beautiful designs to perfection. Until the fifth time. All was going splendidly. Anais was looking cool, calm and collected in a gorgeous midnight blue creation when suddenly the unthinkable happened. She fell. I jumped up; my hands flew to my mouth. I expected the worst. A twisted ankle. A broken ankle. A broken leg?

She was down right in front of me and our eyes locked. For a moment I saw what I think was a flash of distress, maybe even annoyance. This was quickly followed by a twinkle and a smirk. The smirk promptly blossomed into a glamorous smile as she graciously struggled back onto her heels. She continued confidently down the catwalk, her head held high and her smile unwavering. The crowd stood and cheered.

I could not help but wonder: How on earth did she manage to pull this off and with such unfaltering self-confidence?

Hundreds of thousands of articles and hundreds of books have been written about "How to be a Confident Woman." Should you decide to work with a confidence coach, you will have thousands to choose from on- and off-line. You can subscribe to hundreds of on-line confidence building courses. There are even apps now that you can download to help you increase your self-confidence.

> I wrote this book because I hope it will help you become more confident in your abilities as you discover how I deal with my own imperfections and imperfect confidence.

Although I may not be 100% confident myself, I know quite a few women who are. Most of them are French - from there the theme of this book. I thought you might enjoy meeting these women and that you might pick up a few of their confidence secrets along the way. As I have been coaching women for many years, I could not avoid the impulse to add a few "suggestions" of my own to each chapter. I have also included links to useful confidence-building tools that are available on my website, MargarethaMontagu.com. I hope you find these tools useful.

All the links mentioned in the e-book form of this book is available to readers of the printed book at this address: **https://wp.me/P829iE-7d**

Finally, I wrote this book because I feel that not enough emphasis is placed what is one of the most important attributes that a confident woman can have: a great sense of humour. I do not think that a woman can be confident if she cannot laugh at herself. Taking oneself to seriously is a great confidence under-miner. I live in a country, and in a specific region of this country, where women excel at not taking themselves too seriously. Women here laugh often and often uninhibitedly. In this part of the world; a good sense of humour is seen as a valuable and absolutely essential commodity.

About the book and what it can do for you

I host confidence building workshops at our house here in the south of France. My Connect with Horses personal empowerment workshops are based on equine-facilitated experiential learning and equine-guided mindfulness meditation. More than one of our guests has commented on the imperturbable confidence of the local women. They also seem to be under the impression that French women are more confident than women from other nationalities. I am not convinced that this is true. I decided to look into the way French women approach life to see if their approach is different and to see whether this different approach results in them being exceptionally confident. Do keep in mind that this is definitely not a serious piece of research! My main aim is to entertain my readers and if a few pearls of wisdom slip into the text, so much the better. The last chapter does give clear guidelines about how to go about adopting the French approach, but it is the only part of the book that is directive. The rest of the book is full of suggestions, but this is not a step-by-step guide of what to do if you want to boost your self-confidence in five easy steps. I think today's women are perfectly aware that there is no one-size-fits-all solution to confidence building. They know that a technique that works for one person may fail miserably for another. This book puts several possible options before you, enabling you to decide for yourself what will work for you and what not.

Each chapter looks at one possible reason why French women may be markedly more confident. I was not born in France, but I have spent part of my childhood here and most of my adulthood. I have a fair amount of experience of the French savoir-faire. In each chapter, I discuss the subject with one of my French friends. I also share some of my own experiences in each chapter. There may also be a few suggestions of how you can incorporate these strategies into your own life, should you choose to do so.

You may want to start by having a look at a Confidence Quiz or two to determine exactly how confident you are at this moment in time. It is a simple and easy quiz that can be completed in minutes. Even though taking the quiz will not take long, it might just make you think and provide you with a few unexpected insights. It can be accessed online at this address: https://wp.me/P829iE-7d

I have created a Playlist on YouTube that you can listen to while you read. It is a collection of French chansons, sung by French chanteuses. It is called French Women's Confidence Secrets and for you who are reading the printed book, you will find it at my YouTube channel: Margaretha Montagu. Some are older, like Edith Piaf's "Non, je ne regrette rien" and some are more recent like Jennifer's "Tourner ma page. "Some are controversial, like Mylene Farmer's "Je te dis tout," some are full of nostalgia like Barbara Patin's "L'Aigle Noir" and some are just about politically correct like Carla Bruni's "Quelqu'un m'a dit."

To take anything this book too seriously would be counterproductive. My idea is to demonstrate the powerful positive effect that a well-nurtured sense of humour can have on our insecurities. I wish with all my heart that this book will make a difference to your life. I hope that you will benefit from it extensively and that it will motivate and equip you to increase your self-confidence dramatically. Mostly, I hope that you will enjoy reading this book and that next time you find yourself in a challenging situation, you may remember how one of my friends solved a similar problem.

Self-Confidence made Simple was inspired by the Connect with Horses personal empowerment workshops that I host at our 200-year-old farmhouse in the sun-blessed south of France. The workshops are based on equine-assisted personal development and equine-guided meditation and I host these residential workshops with the help of my five super-smart horses. I introduce our guests to a variety of confidence building and stress management methods that they put into practice with the aid of the horses. The farm is easily accessible via five international airports: Bordeaux, Toulouse, Pau, Lourdes and Biarritz. If you would like to meet the horses and go on a virtual visit of the farm, join us at EquineGuidedGrowth.com

About the Author

Dr Margaretha Montagu (MBChB, MRCGP, NLP cert, Counselling cert, Med Hyp Dip and EAGALA cert level 2)

Qualifications, Interests and Experience

You only really need to read this chapter if you wonder what qualifications and experience I have that would make this book a worthwhile read. Right, so I am a medical doctor. I worked as a doctor, mostly with women, for 20+ years. I retired early, partly because of a debilitation eye condition and partly because I became frustrated with the limitations of my profession. I always wanted to own a horse or two, so when I could no longer work as a doctor, I bought Belle de la Babinière, a stunningly handsome Friesian mare and well aware of it. I discovered that horses are like crisps, you can never have only one. I bought Beau de la Babinière, a drop-dead-gorgeous Lusitano stallion. I retrained in equine-assisted experiential learning. I now host Connect with Horses personal empowerment workshops to help women and the odd man to be more confident, to cope better with stress and to communicate more effectively.

As a medical doctor, I have always been interested in stress management. Over the years, I worked in a variety of specialities, including psychiatry, and I came to the conclusion that many diseases have their roots in my patients' inability to handle stress. Instead of treating stress-related and stress-induced illnesses, I decided I would prefer to help my patients prevent stress from causing or worsening disease and ruining their health.

Writings

Somewhere along the line, I started writing. I discovered that being grateful for one's blessings is a great stress management tool. I started writing a gratitude diary. I enjoyed writing so much that I started a blog. I intended the blog to be a shop window showcasing our region, our horses, and our workshops. It quickly became much more. Browsing my blog is indeed a bit like visiting us virtually, but it is also a library filled with articles about confidence building, problem-solving, strengthening relationships, conflict resolving and much more. Eventually, I gathered some of my best blog posts into a book.

My books are Mindfulness and Meditation Options, You ARE Good Enough!, Secure Your promising, purposeful and prosperous Future and I also wrote a book for horse riders who have lost their horse riding confidence: Horse Riding Confidence Secrets. I am currently working on my next book. You can find out more about my other books at MargarethaMontagu.com. Subscribers to my blog's mailing list will be notified when new books are published. During the launch, my mailing list subscribers can usually download a preview of my new book for free, for a limited time. Before I publish the book, I send a free copy to each of the members of my VIP Readers Group for review. If you would like to join this group, please send an e-mail to margarethamontagu@gmail.com with "VIP Readers" as the subject.

On-line Presence

When I researched this book, I collected a huge number of quotes, articles and blog posts. I share these on Pinterest at Margaretha'sMuse, on Twitter at @EquineGuidedMD) and on Instagram as MiaMontagu. I am on Goodreads (MargarethaMontagu) and on LinkedIn (MargarethaMontagu). I have two Facebook pages that I use each as an aide-memoire: Margaretha Montagu's Workshops and Books and Empowering Women.

If you decide to come to one of our personal empowerment workshops, don't forget your fur coat, your highest heels and your tiara! If it sounds as if I have lost the plot, look for this blogpost at my blog on EquineGuidedGrowth.com.

There is something I would like you to know.

Despite all my experience, knowledge and qualifications, I am no different from you. I am far from perfect. I do not always practice what I preach. I do not have the answers to all my questions and I do not have the solutions to all my problems. Like you, I sometimes feel confused and overwhelmed. I am, however, convinced that mindfulness meditation - especially with horses - can make a huge difference to your life. I hope is that the content of this book will help you as much as it helped me.

Chapter 1

Sumptuous Self-Care

Could it be that French women are confident because they know how important it is to make time to look after themselves, physically and mentally?

My friend Christine, born and bred in Gascony in the south-west of France, is one of the most confident women I know. She is also one of the happiest women I know. When I asked her if she thinks confidence has anything to do with self-care, I got this answer:

"But of course! Most certainly! I am confident because I look after myself. I know that when I have to handle a difficult situation, I will be strong enough to do so. If you look after yourself, mentally and physically, you feel confident that you can handle any eventuality. It is perfectly obvious!"

Her answer makes a lot of sense to me. Even though it is perfectly obvious, I know many women who either do not look after themselves. Many do not know how to care for themselves. I thought I would ask my friend how she looks after herself, in case it could be of help to other women who feel less confident. If we do not look after ourselves, we cannot trust ourselves to handle stressful circumstances. Many of my clients look after everyone else first. They often have little time or energy to spend on themselves. Many French women do the exact opposite: they look after themselves before they take care of anyone else.

"You ask how I take care of myself? I will tell you. It is very simple. I look after myself by always putting myself first. How can I help other people if I am not strong enough myself? When I feel strong, I feel confident. When I feel confident, I feel capable of helping others."

I asked each of my friends what they thought is the most important aspect of self-care. Most agreed on a few basics, but I also got a few surprising answers. It is a well-known fact that the women of Gascony (a region in the south-west of France) live long and healthy lives. They live longer and healthier lives than many other women in

France, in Europe and in the rest of the world. I wondered if this had anything to do with self-care. If so, I wondered what self-care secrets the women of the Gers would be willing to share. It seems that looking after yourself physically and mentally may cause you to live a longer and healthier life. It also seems that looking after yourself can make you more confident. To find out if this is true, let's start by asking a few French women how they look after themselves physically.

Sleep

One of my friends answered, "I agree that eating healthily is important, but to me; that is not the most important part of looking after myself. For me, the most important way I look after myself is by getting enough sleep. Sleeping is important, very important. A good night sleep is an incredible confidence booster. I am convinced that it is all a question of priorities, of making time to do what is important to you. I make time to sleep. It boosts my confidence, makes me feel good in the morning, allows my body to restore itself during the night, keeps me looking young...Honestly, there is nothing more effective if you want to look after yourself than to get a few hours of restorative sleep every night. When my children were small, I did not always manage to get enough sleep at night. This was a difficult time for me. As soon as they were old enough, I reverted back to my normal sleeping pattern. Now, all my friends know not to ring me after 10 o'clock at night, nor before 9 o'clock in the morning. It wouldn't be polite, anyway, now would it? If you ring me at 11 o'clock at night, it had better be a life-threatening emergency. Otherwise, I guarantee that I shall be extremely rude.

Naturally, I do not actually sleep from 10pm to 9am. I sleep about eight hours every night, and if I cannot sleep for eight hours at night, I take a nap in the afternoon. After a nap, I wake up refreshed and I can work at twice the speed I did when I was feeling tired. I think one of the reasons the women of Gascony live longer than most other European women is because of their habit to take a short siesta after lunch, every day of the week.

Since sleeping is so important to me, I make sure that I get to sleep in the best possible environment. My bedroom is my refuge. I have spent a lot of time, thought and a fair amount of money decorating my bedroom to my liking. My bedroom reflects my personal preferences. I care little what anyone else thinks of it. It is MY sanctuary. When I walk into my bedroom, I feel all the day's stress lift from my shoulders. I chose a bedroom that faces east, towards the rising sun. Lying in bed watching the sun rise over the rolling hills of the Gascony makes me blissfully happy. I buy the best bed and mattress that I can afford. I replace the mattress regularly, at least every seven years. I was very lucky to inherit my grandmother's bedlinen. I love the feel of the lavender-scented cotton against my skin. I sleep with my window open, except on the coldest of nights, so that I can breathe as much of the unpolluted country air as possible.

In my bedroom, I sleep. I do not eat or watch television or work on my computer. My bedroom is only for the very serious business of sleeping. I sometimes do some yoga first thing in the morning or last thing at night, but I do no other form of exercise in my bedroom. I do not have coffee in bed; I have it on my balcony. I only have pictures of my closest friends and family in my bedroom. The rest of my bedroom walls are covered by some of my grandfather's paintings. Restful scenes, you understand? I keep the room fairly neat and clean. I cannot sleep in a dirty or disorganised room.

For me, sleeping is one of the most effective ways of looking after myself. It is one of the most effective ways of investing in my future. I am sure it is this habit that makes me look so much younger than I am. I am sure that sleeping makes my wrinkles dissolve overnight!"

Diet

Several of my friends mentioned eating healthily and exercising regularly as important aspects of effective self-care. My friend Annie said, "As you know, since we grew up together, eating healthily is very important to me. I do not believe in diets. I never diet. What is the use? Every kilo you lose comes right back and brings a friend to stay. I do keep a careful eye on my weight. From a distance, without getting too involved or too stressed about it. I do not weigh myself every single day. I jump on the scales if my clothes start feeling too tight. If I have put on a couple of kilos, I do something about it immediately. No waiting until next Monday. No last binge before I start. I just get on with it. I simply cut back somewhat. I eat smaller portions. I get a bit more exercise: I walk instead of taking the bus. I make small adjustments along those lines.

I never eat breakfast. I grew up to be the successful and well-balanced person I am today without ever eating breakfast. I know it is against all sensible nutritional advice, but I just cannot face food first thing in the morning. I have a bowl of coffee first thing and then lunch at twelve. My main meal is at lunchtime. I eat something quite light in the evening, a salad or maybe a bowl of soup. That does not mean I do not love food! Of course, I do! All French women love food. The women from Gascony more than most, non? It just means that I believe in moderation in all things. As do most French women, I think. Food and wine matter to French women. Quality is important. Taste and texture are as relevant as looks. You will often see French housewives taking their time to examine the tomatoes on offer at their village market meticulously. Often, they will not buy before they have had a taste. Same goes for cheese. The cheese monger knows he has to offer potential buyers a sliver of the cheese of their choice before expecting them to buy any. If it takes ten slivers before she finds the one she wants, then so be it.

I remember one day I came to have lunch with you. You took your workshop guests to a fresh food market in a nearby village. We used the bits and pieces you bought to make the most decadently delicious lunch. Do you remember? I think we drank that fruity white wine. Your guests seem to appreciate!

Yes, food and wine are very important to us. Especially as a conduit to facilitate relationships. French families still often meet at least once a day to eat together. Extended families meet once a week for Sunday lunch. Sunday lunch usually starts at 12h00 and continues until 18h00. Often, lunch slips into dinner. Family and friends are as essential to us as good food and wine.

We are blessed here in Gascony with the quality and choice of food available to us. Our fruit and vegetables come from our own potagers and orchards. Our eggs come from our own free-range chickens or from one of our neighbours' chickens. Our meat comes from a neighbouring farmer, our water from our mountain springs, our honey from our own bee hives. Have you noticed how the food available follows the seasons? Asparagus is only available in early spring. Strawberries are only available in late spring. Oranges are only available in winter. Go to any village's fresh fruit weekly market, and you will find only fruit and vegetables that are in season, often picked only that morning. I think that it is eating food of this quality that is the secret of the longevity of the Gascon people

Also, many cooks here still only buy enough food for that day's lunch and dinner. Although with the arrival of all these huge supermarkets; this will change, I am sure.

Eating healthily, making sure every morsel contributes to my physical or mental well-being, is the foundation of my self-care program. It is true that I love dark chocolate, the darkest I can get hold of. I don't need a lot of it at any one time; it is so full of flavour. It is also true that I eat a fair amount of rich food, especially at lunch. Rich food is what Gascon gastronomy is all about. I also have a glass or two of our excellent Madiran wine with my lunch. We are very proud of the wine we produce in this region: Madiran, Saint Mont, Cotes de Gascogne and also the brandy, Armagnac. It is a very good thing that you treat all your workshop guest to a tutored wine tasting tour while they stay with you. Our wines are not very well known yet; I am glad that you are introducing people to them. I read a book recently, called The Red Wine Diet. It was written by an English professor, Roger Corder. Prof Corder suggests that our Madiran wine is responsible for our longevity. This, of course; we have known for centuries!

As I do keep moderation in mind, when eating and drinking, my weight varies very little. I am as healthy as...what is it they say in English? I am as healthy as an ox. I still follow my mother and my grandmother's advice. I book into a local mountain spa twice a year, in autumn and in spring for a week-long liquid fast. Does one a world of good, n'est pas? Makes me feel brand-new, clean inside and out. One of my friends told me about a new place we could try this autumn..."

Exercise

Another of my friends had a thing or two to say about exercise: Gym? Over my dead body. I do not believe in making myself suffer. I love to exercise. I love it when my body feels strong and toned, but I prefer to do my exercise somewhere where I can get into contact with nature. Cycling in the park, walking through the woods, running on the beach...that is more my sort of thing. Or a game of tennis. I am seriously into tennis. It means I get my exercise while spending time with my friends. We laugh a lot. We sometimes play well and sometimes badly, but we enjoy each other's company. We barely notice quite how much exercise we are getting. Even so, I am very competitive. I play to win! Afterwards, we have a few glasses of sparkling water together, maybe with a twist of lemon. We have a good natter and put the world to rights.

I also enjoy horse riding because I love horses. Is there anything quite as invigorating as a quick canter on a frosty morning? Looking after my horse also gives me a good work-out. Moving bales of hay, cleaning stables and giving the old girl a good grooming unquestionably makes me exercise muscles that I otherwise rarely use.

Dancing is another favourite way to exercise. I have recently discovered salsa. As I get better at it, I can see that this sort of thing could give one a pretty thorough work-out! It is not just my body that gets exercise. I exercise my mind too, trying to master the sometimes-intricate steps. I also love the music. It keeps me going long after I start to think that I am too tired to keep on dancing. Dancing with a partner makes this way of getting some exercise even more interesting. One has the opportunity to meet new people and make new friends. Definitely an exercise worth the energy investment!

Doing endless repetitions on an instrument of torture in a gym would be mind-numbing. I can't imagine it. Who would want to miss out on all that fresh air? On the glorious sound of birds singing their hearts out? On the heavenly taste of ice-cold water scooped from a mountain stream? The warm feeling of the sun on your face? On the infinite pleasure of swimming naked in a small rock pool at the end of a refreshing run?

I remember my mother taking me for long walks when I was a little girl. We went for walks in the forest behind our house in Normandy in the summer and on the deserted landing beaches in the winter. I remember her teaching me about the seasons, the birds, the weather, the tides...all while walking along at a steady pace until our cheeks were red and our eyes sparkled with happiness. From time to time we would stop to admire a shining shell on the beach, or to investigate a rare footprint on a path in the woods or just to catch our breath. These days, when I go for a walk or a run, I still look about with that same sense of curiosity and awe: I exercise my body while I nurture my soul. I could never get the same benefit in a gym.

I could not possibly do any exercise that I do not enjoy. How do women make themselves do this? And why? I think it is much simpler just to incorporate some exercise in your everyday life. I walk to work; I rarely take the bus. I climb the stairs instead of using the lift. I give the house a good clean once a week. Whenever I can, I take a short walk after lunch and on Sundays I take a long walk with the rest of my family. Sunday lunch is still sacred to most French families. After lunch; we have a short siesta, and then we take a long walk through the countryside. It is not that I am such a paragon of virtue. I have to stay fairly fit because I have to help out my parents in their vineyard most weekends.

Exercise gives me energy, it makes me feel alive, it makes me feel good about myself. It makes me feel confident. It makes me feel attractive."

It is rare to see a lone jogger on a French road, although that may have something to do with French driving habits. One might see two or more joggers together, or a platoon of cyclists or a couple of horse riders. Walkers, especially groups of walkers, are a frequent sight on Sunday afternoon. French drivers know to change their driving habits accordingly. Personally, I would add gardening to the mix. Many French women in the countryside have a potager (vegetable garden) where they grow their own vegetables. Some French women even grow vegetables in pots on their balconies in the cities. Digging over a potato plot is good exercise. One has the added satisfaction of knowing that one will later be able to harvest homegrown potatoes.

Cosmetics

I was especially interested to know what my friend Régine would have to say about self-care. At 77, she is still a beautiful woman. She closely resembles Catherine Deneuve, a very famous French actress. At a similar age, Catherine is still celebrated as one of the most beautiful women in France today. Régine has so much class, such inherent style, such undeniable elegance that she is an inspiration to everyone who knows her. According to Régine:

"As you know, Popette, beauty has no age. Beauty is not superficial. Having said that, I value my skin highly, and therefore I look after it carefully. Admittedly, I inherited some curiously age-defying genes from my mother, but that only counts for about ten percent of what you see today. The rest is due to my skincare regime. My mother taught me the basics, but it was one of my mother's sisters who taught me how to look ten years younger today than I am in reality. My aunt Honoré taught me to take care of my skin, my whole skin, not just the skin of my face, my neck and my arms. I was barely nine when she took me in hand and I have followed her advice these last fifty years." Régine would never, never admit to her real age. As she says, she looks ten years younger than she is, so she effortlessly gets away with it.

"If you want your skin not to show your real age, you need to look after it religiously twice a day. Moisturise, moisturise, moisture. Stay out of the sun. Forget about suntanning lotion and factor 50 sun protection. Wear a hat. Wear gardening gloves in the garden. Wear long sleeves. Watch your diet. Your skin needs protection, but it also needs to be fed. Make sure you eat the right foods to provide your skin with the building stones it needs to rejuvenate itself.

Buy the best skin products you can afford keeping in mind that the most expensive products are not necessarily the best. Buy decent quality make up, learn to put it on properly and adjust your technique to reflect your age. Keep up to date with new discoveries and use them once you are sure of their value.

Remember, Popette, you must apply your make up in such a way that it looks as if you are not wearing any. It is only rarely, in the evening, maybe, that we wear heavier make up. Please, never go without! I cannot repeat that enough. Please, never leave the house without make up. You were born with certain flaws, Popette, you owe it to yourself and to everyone else who have to look at you the whole day long to straighten out those flaws before you leave the house. Keep an eye on yourself during the day and repair any defects frequently, but never in public. Unless you are flirting, there is no excuse for applying lipstick in public.

Plastic surgery? Why not. But only to make small adjustments. If you can see that someone had a face-lift, the operation was a failure. It is much better to figure out how to make the best of what nature has endowed you with, especially as you get older. Aim for elegance, that is my motto. As for going grey naturally, never in a thousand years. There are so very few women who look good with grey hair. The rest of us just look old...and grey. Unkempt. Find a hairdresser who knows what she is doing and make sure you never go more than six weeks without updating your colour. If you want to grow out your hair to see if you are one of the lucky ones, go away somewhere, for six months or for however long it takes. Somewhere where no one knows you.

Look after your hands and look after your nails. I am not a lover of bright nail paint, not for young women and especially not on older women. Have a manicure from time to time and in between manicures, keep your nails well-tended. Nothing shows a women's age quicker than her hands. Look after your teeth too. One of the most beautiful things a woman, of any age, can bestow on an onlooker is a full smile showing healthy teeth. Or to be able to laugh, head thrown back, without having to worry about unsightly fillings or missing teeth." Heaven forbids. Missing teeth.

Clothes

While I was working on this book, I often heard, "Le meilleur accessoire qu'une femme puisse posséder est la confiance en soi." Or, the most valuable accessory a woman can have is confidence in herself. Tourists often comment on the style and elegance of French women. The women of Paris are often cited as an example. No matter what the circumstances, French women seem to manage, often against substantial odds, to remain cool, calm and confident. I asked my friend, Eloise, a Parisian, who always looks as if she has just stepped off a Chanel catwalk, what the reason for this may be.

"Ma chèrie, there is only one answer to this question, and that is clothes. No, en fait, there are two answers: Clothes and shoes. It is the clothes and the shoes that make the woman."

I wasn't entirely convinced. "But Eloise, I know a lot of women who spend small fortunes on clothes and shoes and who never manage to look elegant, never mind all the time. There has got to be more to it than that."

Eloise answered, "Well, I never said the clothes need to be expensive, Chèrie. I think it is more important that a woman knows what suits her and that she wears clothes that make her feel good. Regretfully, that does not always mean that the clothes make her feel comfortable. My mother, and my grandmother for that matter, as well as all my aunts and great-aunts, wore heels whenever they stepped out of their front doors. Not tremendously high heels and lower heels as they got older, but heels nevertheless.

My mother did not believe in following fashion. She might add a little something to an outfit, as a nod to a current fashion trend. My mother wore clothes that suited her body shape and made the best of her attributes. She did not have a dressing room full of clothes. She had a wardrobe with a few good pieces of clothing. She always brought the best that she could afford. If necessary, she postponed a purchase until she had saved enough money to afford it. She used to say, "It is all in the cut. A quality garment will reveal its provenance in the flattering way it fits." Never in a hundred years would she wear anything with the name of the designer visible anywhere or the garment. Never.

My mother, who was not wealthy, nonetheless wore designer clothes and shoes (always Italian and always, always leather). She took good care of each piece. I have inherited some of her clothes. Since we are built along the same lines, I can wear those dresses today and look as stylish as she did fifty years ago. I also inherited her jewelry and here she practised the same adage. She had a few exquisitely beautiful pieces. Most of her jewelry she inherited from my grandmother. The rest she chose with great care, in such a way that my father thought he had made the choice. She did not always wear jewelry. When she did, it always complimented her outfit.

One thinks that it should not need to be said, but I see many young girls today that look as if they have slept with their clothes on. My mother always made sure her clothes were scrupulously clean and ironed. If they needed dry-cleaning, they were dry-cleaned. If they needed mending, they were mended, promptly. If they needed to be washed by hand, they were hand-washed.

My mother taught me was to wear proper underwear. When the time came, she took me to her favourite lingerie shop. I think she had been going to this shop since she was a young girl herself. She seemed to know the owner very well indeed. I found the owner somewhat intimidating, initially. She soon became one of the most important women in my life, as is her daughter today. Because Madame knew the secret of making a bra fit so well that you completely forgot that you are wearing one. En plus, you looked and felt like a princess. My mother used to call lingerie 'the foundation garments." She explained to me that unless the foundation is rock solid, whatever else you add will look not-quite-right. I believe that she was one hundred percent correct. I have found well-made and well-fitting lingerie of invaluable support as I got older. When I was young, beautiful lingerie made me feel sexy and desirable. As I get older, beautiful lingerie makes me feel young.

Another secret my mother shared with me, is to have a proper mirror, with side panels. So that you can see yourself, not just your head, but your whole body from the front and from the back. So many women make the fatal mistake of not checking to see what they look like from behind. I am so annoyed with modern fitting rooms that offer you only a view from the front. How am I supposed to know if I want to buy something if I cannot see myself from behind? Check and recheck, my mother used to say, and check one last time in the mirror by the front door before you leave the house.

The last thing I want to mention is a small, but very important fashion accessory: the scarf. The perfect scarf can transform an outfit. The way you wear the scarf is just about as important as the scarf itself. Parisian women have made tying a scarf into an art. These days, anyone can master this art: there are several videos on YouTube demonstrating different ways to tie a scarf. A scarf can change an average outfit into a superb outfit. Or add a touch of colour. Or hide a wrinkled neck. I think every woman could benefit from having a few scarves in her wardrobe."

I also think one has to look after oneself mentally and in that, my French friends agree with me unanimously. I asked my friend Corinne what looking after herself mentally means to her.

"I believe that a healthy mind lives in a healthy body, so I look after my body. I eat well, I stay fit and strong, I do not smoke, I drink in moderation, I avoid pollution as far as I can. All that sort of things. I look after my mind by spending time with my family. Not just my husband and my children, but also my extended family: our parents, aunts, uncles, cousins...knowing that they are there to help and support me means the world to me. Obviously one can only get as much out of a relationship as you put in, so I nurture these relationships by spending time with these people. As a family, we eat at least one meal together every day. I see other members of my family on Sundays for lunch at my parents'. We talk to each other. We share our day or our week's ups and downs with each other, and when necessary, we help each other. I stay in contact with my family that lives further afield, on Facebook or with Skype...whichever way suits them best. It makes me feel connected. It makes me feel grounded. Rooted in the here and now. Safe. Supported.

I do the same with my friends. Making time for my friends, to talk, to really talk, is nearly as important to me as making time for my family. I have three good friends, friends that I have known since the Maternelle (kindergarten). We make time for each other as often as we can, once a week if possible, once every two weeks, otherwise. Sometimes there is just two of us, sometimes there are four. We have coffee together in the morning, or maybe a glass of white wine after work. We talk. We laugh. Sometimes we cry together.

Maintaining these friendships takes time and commitment, but it is worth it. One reaps the rewards in the sense that one always has a sympathetic listener to hand. Someone that has known me all my life, who knows me inside out. Someone who understands me. It means a lot to me to feel understood. Accepted.

I go to Mass. I would not describe myself as a practising catholic, not exactly, but faith has always been part of my life. I go to confession. Not regularly, but I do go. It is important to me and I am convinced that it helps me stay healthy mentally. Who needs a psychologist when she has a confessor? Also, there is the sense of belonging. Of being part of something bigger. My faith helps me to see the bigger picture and not to get too bogged down in the details. I go to Mass, not only for what I can get from attending, but also for what I can contribute. I am involved in the association that raises money for the renovation and upkeep of our little church. I sing in the church choir.

I feel very strongly about being part of my community. We live in a small 'commune," a village and its surrounding farms. 200 people only. Even though we are few, we know how to party. Every year we organise the village fete together. We have lots of arguments about how things should be done. The older people of the commune think we should do things the way they have been done for the last 200 years. We feel we should make changes. In the process, we get to know each other. We know who lives alone, who struggles financially, who suffers from chronic illness. In the countryside; we look after each other. We know we have to be able to depend on each other. We help each other, expecting nothing in return. Knowing that when the time comes, we will be helped when we need help.

Staying mentally healthy also means keeping my mind fit and free from mental pollution. Adverts, for example. I do not need that sort of mental pollution in my life. I exercise my mind by solving problems, doing puzzles. I am a Sudoku addict, and I do the crosswords whenever I can. In English. I play chess. I read extensively. One can never stop educating oneself. I keep up to date with what is happening in my own country, in the rest of the world. I love a good political debate. I love discussing a good book. I enjoy listening other people's opinions and insights and sharing mine with them. I train my memory by memorising poems.

I nurture my mind by exposing it to beauty. Art. Paintings, sculpture, music...not only of the old masters, but of new talent, new methods of producing art. I spend time communing with nature."

Health

Many other nations accuse the French of being hypochondriacs. There may be some truth in this. The French government has launched a countrywide re-education program to convince the French that they do not need at least five items on a prescription each time they see they doctor for a minor a complaint. Even so, every French woman knows that she feels much more confident when she knows she is fit and healthy.

Maybe it was my awareness of this not-altogether-unfair accusation that caused me to do the exact opposite, to delay seeking medical help when I developed a severe eye disease in my mid-twenties. By the time the disease was properly identified and treated, I had lost a fair amount of my sight. The disease stayed with me, for the rest of my life, necessitating regular operations. I mention it here for two reasons. Firstly, because of the negative influence it has had on my self-confidence. Secondly, because it had taught me a valuable lesson: physical self-care is also about regular check-ups. It is about listening to your body when it is trying to tell you that something is wrong.

Most French women I know are well aware of this fact. They make sure that they never miss a check-up however inconsequential it may seem. The fact that medical care in France is generously subsidised by the government helps. A substantial part of the French budget goes into health care. Regular check-ups also make sense to me as a medical doctor. I firmly believe that preventing illness is better than trying to cure something that already has had time to do lasting damage by the time it is diagnosed. This I learnt the hard way.

Having problems with my eyes severely affects the way I feel about my looks. Regretfully, this eye disease is not the invisible kind. It has left visible scars. Scars that worsened over the years, and with each successive operation. This has left me feeling insecure about the way I look. I suppose this insecurity would just have increased with time, had I not discovered a very useful self-help technique. I would recommend this technique, re-framing, to any woman who, for whatever reason, feels unattractive.

Have you ever noticed how different a painting can look in different frames? This is what re-framing is all about. It is about looking at the same fact or set of facts, in a different way. Or from a different viewpoint. Or through someone else's eyes. There was nothing much that I could do about my unsightly left eye. Or was there?

In my late twenties, I met a French woman who has since become a precious friend and life-long mentor. She helped me to look at myself in the mirror in a different way. She said I should focus on and emphasise my strong points and carefully disguise my weak points. Of course, I already knew how to do this, to a great extent, but how does one disguise an eye as badly damaged as mine?

My friend Solange suggested, before I start re-framing and re-labelling anything, that I tune in to my inner critic. She wanted to know many times recently I allowed my insecurity about how I look hold me back from doing something that I really wanted to do. I had to admit that I avoid doing anything that would put me in the limelight. She said, "The negative way you think people see you determines the way you feel about yourself. It limits your potential and your progress." Aherm. Guilty as charged.

She continued, "Many of us suffer from covert perfectionism, especially where our appearance is concerned. This limits our ability to enjoy ourselves. Judging and criticising yourself destroys your self-confidence. You should try to become more aware of your inner critic. That little voice in your head that says things like "You eye looks awful! You will scare little children on the street!" This is the voice of your internal critic. Your inner critic wants to protect you by not exposing you to danger or by not letting you take "inappropriate risks." Often those warnings were apt when you were younger. They are no longer relevant, yet they still influence your actions.

Your inner critic gives you a running commentary of how it thinks other people see you and react to you. It suggests a variety of things that could go wrong because you do not have perfect looks. It can be extremely damaging to your self-esteem. It is essential to identify this little voice, acknowledge it and understand that it is only trying to protect you from physical or mental pain. You can then choose to turn the volume down. Or you can balance your inner critic with an inner coach, by using affirmations."

I find it very difficult to identify my inner critic. Usually, by the time I realise that my actions are the direct result of my inner critic's over-protectiveness, it is too late. My dear friend suggested I keep a diary. This was not easy for me. I was not much of a diary writer. (I have since seen the error of my ways.) I decided to try it for two weeks, more to please her than because I thought it would work. When I became aware that I was criticising myself, I noted these negative thoughts in a little notebook. I hate to admit it, but after a week, I did start to see patterns emerge in the way I was thinking and talking to myself.

According to my friend-turned-mentor, "The next step in dealing with negative self-talk is to confront the damaging thoughts that you have identified while keeping a diary. You should look at every thought you wrote down and rationally challenge it. When you challenge negative thoughts, you will discover that some of these thoughts are unrealistic. Some have no substance to them. Everyone can choose how they want to see themselves, the situation they find themselves in, a challenge they have to face or an opportunity that comes their way. You can choose to focus on potential solutions. Or you can choose to be overwhelmed by difficulties. When you become aware of your inner critic, it becomes clear that judgemental thinking, painful memories and misinterpretations can damage your self-esteem.

Look at yourself through someone else's eyes. See yourself through my eyes. I hardly notice your bad eye. Looking at yourself from a different viewpoint or seeing yourself through another's eyes can be an eye opener. Re-frame your view of yourself. Re-framing is a simple process. The idea is to alter someone's perception of a person or an event, resulting in a different emotional response.

Looking at yourself through someone else's eyes can help you choose to give greater significance to the positive viewpoint. We usually tend to focus on what went wrong. We beat ourselves up about it, instead of learning from our mistakes. We are often blind to our own potential and to the possibilities and opportunities that come our way. We are more aware of our own weaknesses than our strengths.

By re-framing an event, you choose what the event will mean to you. You decide how you are going to respond to it emotionally."

"Would that not be a form of denial?", I wonder aloud.

"No," she answers, "it isn't. You don't deny that something has happened. You just look at the event from a different angle. You decide to accept the possibility that you have a choice in how you respond emotionally. You can choose to feel irritated. You can choose to feel sorry for yourself. Or you can focus on what you have learnt from an experience.

We do not have to feel impotent. We can choose how we allow circumstances and events to influence us. We can change our interpretation of what happened, and we can adjust our response to this interpretation.

When we re-frame and re-label, we take control of how we are going to react. We consciously decide not to get frustrated, angry or resentful. We decide not to judge or criticise ourselves and not to judge or criticise others. Our self-confidence remains intact. We all have to cope with disappointments and difficulties from time to time. We all deal with difficulties and disappointments in our own unique way. Some people go into denial and continue as if nothing happened. Others withdraw from the world. Yet others see each challenge as an opportunity to excel.

So it is also with your eye. You can choose to see only the damaged eye or you can choose to emphasise the undamaged eye. Go see your hairdresser and ask for a haircut that makes your good eye more visible than your bad eye. Consult a make-up artist who can teach you the subtle art of emphasising your good eye while making your bad eye less obvious. Wear bold, sparkling jewelry in the ear closest to your good eye. Get a tattoo on your right cheek. You see, when you are willing to lose sight of your frustration and look at this as a problem to be solved, possible solutions present themselves.

Do not forget to celebrate the fact that you still have one fairly good eye. Many blind people would give anything to be in your shoes. Do not forget to be grateful for what you have. Look after your good eye very carefully and make sure that you rest your bad eye as often as needed."

I took these very wise words to heart.

Self-care is important. Compassionate self-care can increase your self-confidence dramatically. Self-care involves taking intentional action to care for your physical, mental and emotional health. Having read all of the above, you may feel a bit intimidated. Don't be. If you are not quite sure how well you take care of yourself, there is a Self-care Quiz on my website that you may want to have a look at. You can access it online at https://wp.me/P829iE-7d.

If you have been neglecting yourself for a while, I suggest that you start small. Start by making small changes. Set yourself a simple goal to start with. When you have achieved this goal, set another. The last chapter in this book discusses goal setting in depth.

Treat yourself with compassion. Self-care is a challenge for many people, especially for survivors of physical and mental abuse. Be patient with yourself. Rome wasn't built in one day. Nor was Paris, for that matter.

If you are too stressed, you can decide, "I will meditate for 10 minutes every morning."

If you want to get more exercise, set a small but specific goal. "I will go for a 20-minute walk in the park on Mondays, Wednesdays and Fridays during my lunch hour."

To lose weight, "I will stop snacking between meals."

To eat more healthily, you may choose to: "Eat one piece of fruit a day." Or you may opt to: "Keep a food diary for a week."

If you suffer from insomnia, you could improve your sleep hygiene: "I will go to bed every night during the week by 23h00."

Setting boundaries may involve: "I will not be available to everyone 24/7. I am going to screen my phone calls."

Balancing your life may include: "I will meet my friends once a week for a coffee at our favourite coffee shop."

If you need to recharge your batteries, you can decide, "I will make a date with myself once a week to spend an hour doing something I enjoy."

Looking after yourself is an investment in your future.

Remember my friend Anais? Let's see if we can figure out how Anais managed to stay so calm and confident under such pressure. I have a vague suspicion that it has something to do with the fact that Anais knows exactly who she is and what she wants. In the next chapter, I talk to Anaïs about identity and how a well-defined and positive self-image can help anyone feel more self-assured.

Chapter 2

Choosing and Changing your Identity

My understanding of self-confidence is simple. You are a confident person when you know you can handle any challenge that comes your way. You know that you are wise enough, competent enough, experienced enough and clever enough to cope with most situations. Knowing this would imply that you know yourself well. You are intimately acquainted with your strengths as well as your weaknesses. Not all of us are.

Many French women seem to have an unfair advantage in this regard. Many of the confident French women I am privileged to call my friends have a very clear understanding of who they are. Ask any of them. You will immediately, in no uncertain terms, without any hesitation, and with complete confidence be told that they are, first and foremost, 100% French. They are Gascons (from the Gascony region of France). They are from such and such a village where their family has lived for the last five centuries, at least. Go ahead and ask them how they would describe themselves. They will tell you that as French women, they are independent, courageous and highly intelligent. As Gascon women, they are loyal, spontaneous, generous and full of joie de vivre. As a Garreau, Maillard or Ducasse women, they are intelligent, determined and sympathetic. Knowing exactly who you are and what you are capable of can be a great advantage in a stressful situation.

I asked my friend Anaïs, who is serenely confident in all situations, how she manages to be so sure of herself at all times. She explained:

"If I am confident, it is because I know who I am. I grew up in a small village in the Gers. I was brought up by both my parents. Mostly by my mother, as Papa was always busy with the farm. I did not see that much of him. I grew up surrounded by both sets of grandparents, my mother's sister and of her children and my father's brothers and their children. In the same small village, my grandfather's family lived. He had two sisters. Their children and grandchildren lived in our village too.

I had no problem when I was a teenager to figure out who I am. I am Anaïs K, daughter of Jacques and Edith K, granddaughter of Babette and Jean K, sister of Lucas K and cousin of Thierry, Amelie, Marie-Claire and Genevieve.

Our family has lived in the village for many generations, so I was also Anaïs K. from Fenton, a village in the Gers. A Gerçois, born and bred and proud of the fact. Gerçois people are often convivial, hospitable, passionate, intense and sometimes short-tempered. Knowing this, I also had a good idea of what sort of person I am.

The men and women of my family took part in all the wars that ravaged in this region. We fought in the war against the Black Prince in the 13th century and in all the wars since then, including the Great War. Several members of my family died during the second world war – both in the front lines and in the service of the Resistance. We are known and respected in the region because of the sacrifices we made. So I know I come from courageous, tenacious and strong-willed stock. This helps me when I find myself in challenging situations.

My family has farmed this land for centuries. They were, and are, careful and conscientious farmers. They took good care of the land so that their sons and grandsons would benefit from their investment. We are a family of wine makers. I grew up close to the land. I knew from an early age that there would be a place for me on the farm for the rest of my life.

I am a vigneron's daughter. I learnt the art from my father, my grandfather and my uncles. I also learnt from my mother and my aunts, who looked after the finances and marketing of our wine business. I always loved this way of life, the countryside, the Gers and the people who live here. As you know, my brother is today a lecturer at Pau university, so I took over my father's vineyard. The part of the farm that my father inherited from my grandfather was small. My father managed to buy more land and planted more vines. This means I make a comfortable living doing something I adore and have loved since I was a child. Since most of my family still live in the village, I never have to go far if I need advice about anything! Sometimes we disagree because I want to use newer methods of wine producing. If they give me too much hassle, I just remind them that they used to be called rebel-vignerons in their youth!

Living in a village surrounded my own family meant that I always had friends close by. Several of my cousins were the same age as I was, or a couple of years older or younger. I have heard it said that one's cousins are often the first friends one has in life. That was definitely the case in my life. We were all blessed with the same genes. We had many physical and mental characteristics in common. Many mannerisms too. It not only gave me a sense of who I am but also a sense of belonging. As some of my cousins were older than I was, I always had a choice of role models. Most of my childhood friends also had a clear understanding of who they were and what they were good at. We took this knowledge for granted.

My mother saw early on which way the wind was blowing. She realised that my brother was not interested in taking over the farm. He wanted to study and become an academic. She realised that I was the one who wanted to become a winemaker, so she prepared the way for me. I cannot say that there wasn't any opposition when my father and uncles realised a woman was going to take over my father's estate. I did have a few things going for me: I am a vigneron's daughter, wine making is in my blood. I have learnt everything there is to know about wine making from my father and my uncles. I learnt about the finances and marketing of wine from my mother and aunts. I had the enthusiasm my brother lacked. Eventually, I won the battle. My generation's women have to prove that women can make wine as well as any man. The next generation's women will be accepted as equals, if not better winemakers than men.

You see, the fact that I know exactly who I am makes me confident of my abilities. This knowledge has served me well, making my own way in life and getting to do what I love to do.

I do not know if this type of confidence, based on a clear understanding of one's own identity, is exclusive to Frenchwomen. What I do know is that it has helped several women of my generation convince our own families, and the public at large, that we are as good at making and selling wine as our fathers and forefathers were."

Anaïs is right. It is unlikely that only Frenchwomen have this type of confidence. The problem is that many girls grow up in cities these days, far from their grandparents, their uncles, their aunts and their cousins. They do not even see their parents that often. Both parents are usually working. This is happening in French cities too. No everyone was lucky enough to grow up in a small village. Not everyone grew up in the presence of an extended family. Not everyone had inspiring role models of different ages in their immediate vicinity. Not everyone received unwavering support from their family. I would venture to say that this scenario is more and more the exception rather than the rule. Even in France, things are changing. Young families are leaving the villages where they grew up. They leave the safety and security of their families behind. They are attracted by the promise of work in French cities.

What can you do if you too did not grow up with this in-bred knowledge of who you are and where you come from? There is a way you can develop this sort of confidence. You can create your own identity

It has been said that life is less about finding yourself and more about creating or recreating yourself. This makes sense to me. I think that having a strong sense of your own unique identity definitely affects how confident you are.

If you are not French, and you did not have the benefit of a "French" upbringing, you can still be confident about who you are. Just like Anaïs. You were not born into a family that can trace its family tree back to William the Conqueror. That does not matter. You can create your own identity and so establish the same imperturbable confidence as many French women seem to have. It is perfectly possible. If you suffer from severe self-doubt, do not despair.

Mind you, defining your identity is hard work. It helps not to get too uptight about it. Revealing weaknesses that you did not know you had can help you take these weaknesses into account and enable you to make better decisions in crisis situations.

Many of the suggestions I make in this book are based on tried-and-tested methods I discovered by reading books from authors like Stephen Covey, Jack Canfield, Dale Carnegie, Anthony Robbins and many more. I studied the work of Prof. Jon Kabat-Zinn, Prof Mark Williams, Dr. Robert Emmons and several others. You will find a list of my favourite books in the bibliography section of this book. The methods I have included in this book are all extremely effective. I have used them myself, and I have successfully used them with many of my patients and clients.

Defining Your Identity

Suggestion 1

My first suggestion would be to take a really good look at your strengths and weaknesses. Grab a pen and a piece of paper (or open a file on your computer – whatever works best for you) and make two lists.

Make a list of your strengths.

Start with simple things, like "I bake a decadently delicious chocolate cake." From simple talents, move on to more advanced strengths:

- I am a good listener.
- I have a great sense of humour.
- I do what I said I would do.

Think back over the past few hours, days, weeks and months. List everything you did well. Did you receive any compliments? Did someone thank you for something you did? Take your time to make this list.

Make a second list of your weaknesses. It is usually much easier to make this list than the first one. We are much better at criticising ourselves than we are at complimenting ourselves.

- I procrastinate.
- I am easily distracted.
- I am always late.

If you find your second list is much longer than your first list, add a strength for every weakness you have added. This happens to just about everyone. Most people find it easier to remember their failures rather than their success. This is not about beating yourself up. It is about finding out who you are. It is about identifying your useful characteristics and your less useful characteristics. If you need help, talk to someone whom you trust and who has known you for a long time. Ask them what they think your strengths and weaknesses are. Think carefully about what they have to say. It would be even more useful to talk to more than one person and compare their suggestions. Only add the strengths and weaknesses that everyone agrees about, including you. Don't be too hard on yourself. You are only human after all.

You will also benefit from having a good look at your values and your beliefs. Your values and beliefs significantly influence your attitude and behaviour. They serve as guidelines that you follow without thinking in most situations that you find yourself in. Our values are often discernible in the way we live our lives. Everyone has their own set of values and beliefs. You may value freedom of speech. You may value your independence. I value integrity, and I value personal accountability. We are all different.

Values and beliefs are two different entities. Your values are a set of ideas and convictions that help you distinguish between "right" and "wrong." Beliefs are statements that you believe are true, based on your past experiences. Values and beliefs are intricately intertwined because your beliefs determine how you develop and define your values.

To help you get started, you will find a list of some of the most common values people hold below. From this list, choose the ten values that are the most important to you. You can do an on-line search for more values, if you do not find all ten of your most important values here. You will find lists of 500+ distinctly different values when you make a "list of personal values" Google search.

Accountability, abundance, accomplishment; achievement, adventure, altruism, ambition, approval, assertiveness, balance, beauty, belonging, boldness, calmness, certainty, change, closeness, commitment, compassion, composure, consistency, control, determination, diligence, discipline, empathy, energy, entertainment, enthusiasm, fairness, fidelity, focus, growth, happiness, harmony, independence, inspiration, integrity, meaning, nonconformity, openness, patience, passion, peace, positivity, prosperity, prudence, reliability, resourcefulness, security, self-respect, sensitivity, status, thankfulness, thoroughness, thoughtfulness, trust, understanding, unity, vision, wisdom.

You are defining your own identity by doing this exercise, so be honest with yourself. Take it seriously, but not too seriously. Celebrate your strengths and indulge your weaknesses.

Suggestion 2

My next suggestion is that you make a list of your achievements. List every achievement, big or small, relevant or irrelevant. List your qualifications, your decorations, your awards. These are important. List also the things that you have achieved that you may not consider important.

- I have read through the Bible.
- I have learnt how to ride a horse.
- I have survived my divorce.

Are you starting to see how this may work? At the end of this exercise, you want to create a personal mission statement, defining who you are. You can construct a statement like this one: "I am someone who values loyalty, trustworthiness and efficiency. I can survive emotional trauma and come out stronger on the other side. When I set my mind to mastering a new skill, like horse riding, I persevere until I can do it. My good sense of humour helps me to keep things in perspective." Take your time. If you get stuck, ask other people what they think your greatest achievements are. You may be surprised at the number and variety of their responses!

Suggestion 3

Suggestion 3 involves making a list of things that you love and that you love to do. List anything that you would be happy to do for hours on end. Anything that makes time stand still. List anything that you would happily do even if you were not paid to do it. You may make one list about the things you love. For example, you may love books, summer sunsets, freshly-made coffee and freshly-baked bread. Your other list should be about things that you love to do, like browsing vintage shops, cooking a recipe for the first time, walking in the woods, shopping during the sales...anything that makes your heart sing.

Making these lists is easy and enjoyable. I usually suggest to our guests that they include things that they enjoy doing for other people. What do you love to do, or would love to do, for other people, for your community, for your country and for your environment?

Suggestion 4

Suggestion 4 is optional. If you are just trying to figure out who you are, if you are trying to define your identity for the first time accurately, you can skip this step. If you are facing a new challenge or unavoidable change and you want to adjust your identity to fit your new circumstances, then this step is for you.

I grew up knowing more or less exactly who I am. I also had a good idea of what I wanted to do with my life. From an early age; I was aware that I am a "De Klerk." My father's family, especially my aunt Angela, shaped my identity. She left me in no doubt about my abilities. Or about my weaknesses! My aunt Angela was one of my earliest role models. One of the things I most admired about her was her gardening skills. She loved roses. Over the years she planted hundreds of rose bushes of all shapes and varieties on the farm she and her husband owned. She turned her passion into a lucrative business. She sold roses for wedding receptions. I remember asking her how she managed to become such a proficient gardener. I was a young woman - just married - and keen to create a garden of my own on our farm in Normandy. She simply said: "It is very easy. Just follow your instinct. You are a "De Klerk." All "De Klerk" women know how to garden. Just get on with it."

So I did.

For most of my career, I was a medical doctor. For some 20 odd years, being a doctor was an essential part of my identity. How big a part of my identity, I only discovered when I had to retire from medical practice due to serious eye problems.

Being a doctor provides you with an instant identity. It provides you with expectations to live up to and if you do, the respect of your patients. For more than 20 years, my identity was based on these premises. When I retired, I felt lost. If I wasn't a doctor anymore, what was I? What was I going to do with myself for the rest of my life?

At this point, I worked through the exact suggestions I mention above, one by one. I had a good look at who I was after 20 odd years of medical practice. I made a list of my strengths and my weaknesses, my values and my beliefs, my qualifications and my professional experience. I made a list of what I loved doing. I wondered how I could possibly combine it all to create a new career for myself. I realised I would have to create a new identity to support my choices, within the confines of my eye disease.

If you are at a similar point in your life, you may find this suggestion useful too. Start by answering this question: "If I can do anything that I want to do, if I did not fear failure and I had no financial constraints, what would I do?" Answering this question can give you a clear idea of who you want to be and what you want to do.

Suggestion 5

Having worked through the suggestions above, you may now be wondering where to go from here. This is where resources, research and re-education come in.

When I did this exercise, a long-forgotten deep-set desire from my childhood stirred. I had always wanted to own a horse. I had always dreamed of owning one or better yet, a whole herd of horses! While I was working as a doctor, there was never enough time to ride, never mind to own and to look after a horse. I started reading and researching the care of horses. I soon discovered that it was going to be an expensive undertaking. A steady income was going to be essential. I came back to my lists. I tried to find a way to use my education and experience that would allow me to earn enough to make my dream come true.

During my research; I came across a new discipline: equine-assisted psychotherapy and experiential learning. This looked like the perfect solution: Equine-assisted psychotherapy and experiential learning would enable to combine my knowledge (I had worked for many years in psychiatry) with horse ownership. But I needed qualifications and experience before I could work in this field. It took me three years to get my EAGALA level II certificate. (Equine-Guided Growth and Learning Association)

It was hard work and I could not have managed it on my own. In addition to research and re-education, one also needs adequate and appropriate resources. Support is essential. You are going to need someone to talk to…It is useful to identify and to set up an extensive support system before you start making changes. If you can afford it or have access to it, the professional help of a coach, a counsellor or a psychotherapist can be invaluable. If not, you can devour self-help books, like I did. There is an enormous choice available on- and off-line. By identifying your resources, you are setting yourself up for success.

Most French women are born with an extensive family support system already in place. They learn from early on how to nurture and maintain these relationships. It is only natural that they should feel more confident than the average woman with this sort of back-up. If you do not have a support system yet, now would be a good time to start creating one. There are many books available that can help you. In the bibliography section of this book, you will find some examples.

Suggestion 6

To get a clear idea of who you are and benefit from the confidence that this knowledge can give you, I suggest you get rid of your limiting beliefs and invalid excuses. Getting rid of limiting beliefs takes energy and effort. The best way to go about it is to break up the task into several small but significant steps.

We all have an extensive library of convictions that we carry within ourselves. These convictions are beliefs, views, ideas, principles, conclusions, judgements and decisions that we that have made about ourselves. Our beliefs are often limiting, inaccurate and unrealistic. Luckily, we can easily change our beliefs. After all, we used to believe that the earth is flat and that the sun revolves around the earth. We no longer believe this. We changed this belief when we were confronted with evidence to the contrary.

Your beliefs influence your interpretation of events and circumstances. What we believe about who we are and about what we can do influence our interpretation of reality. Our beliefs influence not only our interpretation of events, but also our decisions, our emotional response and our actions. We filter what we see and what we hear. We empower our beliefs to act as self-fulfilling prophecies. If you are convinced that you are stupid, you will probably not want to make an effort to master a new skill, which will certainly not make you any more accomplished! Your beliefs dictate your actions. The result of your actions proves to you that your beliefs are true. Over time, your limiting beliefs become so ingrained that they are difficult to identify and even more difficult to eliminate.

Our beliefs don't always reflect our true identity. We may have created a "false" identity based on past events and experiences.

You may believe that you are not intelligent or talented enough to be successful at anything. If you believe this about yourself, you may have convinced yourself that any attempt to change is a waste of time. If you do somehow manage to overcome your self-doubt and start working toward a specific goal, the slightest glitch will convince you that your original belief was correct: You are just not intelligent or talented enough to do this.

To eradicate limiting beliefs about who you are, you first need to identify these beliefs. When you have identified your limiting beliefs, you will need to question the validity of these beliefs. Once you have identified your limiting and unrealistic beliefs, you can change them. You can replace them with more realistic beliefs.

What do you believe about yourself? Are you smart or stupid or of average intelligence? Are you attractive, ugly or ordinary? Are you an introvert, an extrovert or a bit of both? Are you lucky or unlucky? Each of your answers to these questions is either a limiting or empowering belief. It is based entirely on your perception of yourself and on your interpretation of past experiences. Once we firmly believe something about ourselves, we tend to ignore all evidence to the contrary. We focus only on those events that reinforce that limiting belief. Our limiting beliefs are so much part of who we are that they can be very difficult to identify.

Most of our beliefs about ourselves are formed during our childhood. During your childhood, every time you made a mistake, you may have been told that you are stupid. We tend to accept what we were told about ourselves during our childhood. You may have been told, "You are lazy/stupid/clumsy/ugly" or "You are clever/talented/creative/beautiful." As adults, we assume that because we once react in a certain way, we will always react in this way. In reality, our limiting beliefs may be based on complete misinterpretations of past events.

Can you change your beliefs about yourself? Yes, you most certainly can. Even if you have believed a specific set of suppositions for many years, you can adjust or change these beliefs. The first step is to become consciously aware of the belief and its impact on your life. Once you have identified a specific limiting belief about yourself, you can choose a more realistic belief to replace it. You can use an affirmation to replace a limiting belief. Affirmations can help you define your identity more accurately. An affirmation is a realistic statement that you make about yourself. Using affirmations to change limiting beliefs is not difficult. We use affirmations all the time, intentionally or unintentionally. You may wake up in the morning, jump out of bed and exclaim "It is going to be a great day!" – a positive affirmation. This might not work on a Monday. Or you may drag yourself out of bed awhile whimpering "I feel rotten." This is a negative affirmation. Although it might actually be true, especially on a Monday.

When you catch yourself thinking something negative about yourself, you can use an affirmation to counteract this negative thought. You may find yourself thinking "I can't do this. I'm just not smart enough." You can create an affirmation to counter this destructive way of thinking. For example, you might say to yourself "I am smart enough to handle this. I will keep at it however long it takes." I some people find that a quote speaks to them more eloquently than a statement they made up themselves. It helps to write your affirmation down and to repeat it frequently until it becomes part of you. Commit to repeating your affirmation to yourself for at least 30 days. If the limiting belief that you are trying to change is more complicated and long-standing, you may need more than 30 days.

Suggestion 7

A mission statement is an inspiring and motivating statement that sums up exactly who you are. It serves as a guide when you have to make difficult decisions and when you find yourself in challenging situations.

It takes time to create a mission statement that fits. It often needs many rewrites before it finally feels like your own. It could take days, weeks or months…The most effective mission statements are short and to the point. A concise paragraph that provides you with clarity, direction and a sense of purpose is all that is required. Sometimes a single sentence is enough.

Some experts recommend 50 words or less. I think it is important to fully articulate the vision you have of yourself and of what you want for your future. The number of words you use is less important.

Every mission statement is unique. You may want to incorporate those specific skills, qualifications and qualities that you had identified when you listed your strengths and achievements. Also add anything that will have a significant positive impact on the quality of your life. You may want to include the ten values that you consider particularly important and want to develop further. Your mission statement will give you an accurate impression of your identity at this moment in time. Knowing who you are and what you want dramatically increases your self-confidence.

To help you formulate your personal mission statement, you may want to use these prompts:

"To ... [what you want to achieve] ... so that ... [reasons why it is important]. I will do this by ... [actions and skills you will need]."

"I value ...[fill in your most important values]... because ...[reasons why these values are important to you]. Accordingly, I will ...[how you will live by these values]."

"To live each day with ...[choose up to three values or principles]... so that ...[what living by these values will achieve]. I will do this by ...[actions you will take to ensure you live by these values]."

I review my mission statement at least once a year, to see what minor changes and adjustments are needed. A personal mission statement should act as a reminder of who you are and what you want now, so in the future, it may need regular adjustment. A mission statement is a work in progress. It will continue to evolve as you gain further insight into who you are and as you face new challenges.

You may also want to create a vision board. You can download a free guide on how to create a vision board from my website. Click on this link to download your free vision board guide here: https://wp.me/P829iE-7d

You can change the way you interpret events and experiences by changing who you think you are.

When I decided to make a career change, I had to redefine my identity. Some people would call it re-invention. I would not go that far. I simply adjusted my self-image to fit my new lifestyle. It was more of a readjustment than a reinvention. I talked everything through with my father and with my step-mother, Shirley. I was worried that they would disapprove of my decision to change careers, especially as my father had paid for my education. They did not. On the contrary, they understood and supported my decision. My father said, and his words will stay with me for the rest of my life, "There is only one thing every parent wants for his/her child, and that is happiness. I want you to be happy."

This is the longest chapter in this book. In my opinion, it is also the most important. Having a clear-cut understanding of who you are, provides you with a solid foundation to build on. If you lack confidence in yourself, you can start rebuilding your confidence by laying a strong foundation - an unambiguous understanding of who you are.

To consolidate what you have learnt in this chapter, I suggest you look up this article online and listen to some of the talks: 10 Mind-Blowing TED Talks On How To Be Confident about sustainable confidence-building. Knowing who you are and what you can and cannot do will also help you set realistic boundaries. Well-defined boundaries will help you look after yourself. I have noticed that French women are very good at looking after themselves, in various different ways. They seem to know the secret of how to balance what other people need from them with what they need themselves. In the next chapter, I talk to my friend Beatrice about balancing responsibilities and about aiming for moderation in all things.

Chapter 3

Balancing Act

We hear so much about stress these days. We hear about how dangerous too much stress is for our physical and mental health. We hear about friends having heart attacks. We hear about family members getting cancer because they could not handle the stress in their lives. We hear about breakdowns and about burnout.

I have seen what stress can do to my patients physical and mental health. I have seen it destroy good, solid relationships. I have seen it destroy friendships when friends were most needed. I have seen it destroy marriages made in heaven. I have encountered many of the diseases caused and worsened by stress in my practice. I have worked with my patients to conquer this invisible enemy before they suffered permanent damage to their health. I have coped with the fall-out after stress-related and stress-induced incidents. I have helped family members of patients deal with new challenges resulting from such incidents.

Stress is unavoidable. A certain amount of stress is even essential for peak performance. But too much stress can be extremely harmful in the short- and in the long-term.

All this can be avoided by balancing the various demands made of us – something most French women I know are quite good at.

It seems to me that French women who manage their stress levels effectively have mastered the art of time management. One of the most important skills needed for successful time management is the ability to say no, without feeling the need to apologise or to explain.

I have a French friend who excels in stress management. This does not mean that she is never stressed. It just means that she is able to deal with the stress that comes her way. I think I have discovered her secret. It is all about balance.

Beatrice is an attractive woman in her late fifties. She is always beautifully but simply dressed. She loves walking and does a lot of it. She is consequently fit, trim and healthy. She loves cooking, she loves entertaining, and she loves combining these two passions. She is insatiably curious. She is always eager to learn and develop new skills. She is a great conversationalist. She possesses the ability to make everyone she talks to feel like the most important person in the room. She loves animals and has an enviable knack with them. She dotes on her children. All are grown up now and have made their way in the world. She speaks excellent English and Spanish.

Beatrice left France to go and work in one of France's old colonies thirty years ago. This was no small or simple undertaking. Thirty years ago, travelling to the other side of the world was much more challenging. It took much longer than it does now. Even though it takes her twenty-four hours to travel to France, she still comes back regularly to see her mother. Beatrice has recently bought an old farmhouse in the French countryside that she is currently renovating. With her husband, she also owns a house in their adopted country. Since her children have left home, she started a business selling European products to New-Zealand shop owners.

Beatrice does not let the stress that all this travelling, owning properties in different countries, worries about her mother and children and running an international business get her down. Quite on the contrary. She is a vivacious, caring and generous woman and a phenomenal cook to boot. She always makes time for other people's problems. She offers practical help whenever she can.

How does she manage it? I have long wondered about this myself. We have been friends for many years. I have seen her cope with emergencies that involved dropping everything and flying to the other side of the world. On more than one occasion. I have seen her cope with the stress of looking after elderly parents. I have seen her manage financial challenges. I have seen her stand up to illness and defend her right to good health. I have seen her deal with marital difficulties.

Through all these hard times, her confidence never wavered.

She knows how to look after herself, mentally and physically. She knows how to say no when she needs to. Even so, there is more to her steady self-confidence, her characteristic French poise, her eternal elegance and her bubbling joie de vivre.

Beatrice aims for balance. She aims to do everything in moderation. Epicurus said nearly two centuries ago: 'Be moderate in order to taste the joys of life in abundance.' Beatrice makes time for her husband, for her friends, for her family, for her business, for her hobbies and for herself - all in equal measure.

In my own life, I have not always been as successful in creating balance. During the seven years I was studying medicine, there was little time for anything but my studies. I spent the first seven years after graduation learning my trade. The next seven years I constantly retrained as my eye problems dictated what sort of work I could do. I did my best to make time for my husband, my friends and my family. I did my best to look after myself, but still spent most of my time working. Towards the end of my thirties, this lifestyle became unbearable and unsustainable. I was not happy. My life was completely out of balance. I finally realised that I would have to make some drastic changes. My eye problems were getting worse, and I was dissatisfied with my job.

I have always loved horses and since I was a child, dreamed of one day owning one of my own. I can vividly remember the exact place and time I fell in love with a horse. I was about ten years old. We lived in a small village, not far from Versailles. The village is about thirty minutes from the heart of Paris, in France. My brother and I walked to school every morning. There was a meadow that we were supposed to avoid at all cost. Being the adventurous children we were, we never did. We climbed through the fencing and cut across the field, every morning. It shortened our walk with at least 10 minutes, especially appreciated on freezing cold winter mornings.

We were walking across the meadow on a cold and misty winter morning, with frost crunching under our boots, when I first came face to face with a horse. It was a pitch-black and bad-tempered stallion. This was an expected encounter, as this field had never been occupied before. It was clearly the reason why we had been told to walk around the field. Said stallion was not impressed by finding unexpected intruders on his private property. He took one angry look at us, pawed the ground and promptly charged. I could feel the drumming of his hooves on the frozen earth through my feet. He came at us at full gallop.

I think I cried something like "Sauve qui peut!" Quite unnecessarily, as my brother was already running hell for leather towards the fence. With my own heart beating desperately in my ears I followed suit. I dived through the fence to the relative safety of a deep and very muddy ditch.

Scrambling up, I turned to look around. What I saw took what little breath I had left away completely. He stood there on his back legs, furiously pawing the air. His was tossing his mane and swishing his tail. I was scared, but I was also mesmerised by his beauty.

Apart from occasional meetings like the one above, horses were regretfully not part of my childhood. Nor of my early adulthood. I was too busy studying, dating and getting married. I had always wanted to be a doctor. I especially wanted to help women, so I started specialising in Obstetrics and Gynaecology. Not long after, disaster struck.

That day, I spent the morning assisting in gynaecological operations. By the end of the morning, it felt as if someone was repeatedly stabbing me in my left eye with a red-hot knife. It was so painful that I fainted. I was immediately admitted to the very same hospital where I had just that morning been operating on patients. Thus began a twenty-five-year struggle to preserve my sight. A battle that has resulted in complete loss of sight in my left eye and less than 50% vision in my right eye. Luckily, my sight deteriorated gradually, over many years, giving me time to adjust. As I could no longer operate, I changed to Psychiatry, a discipline I found as fascinating as Gynaecology. I eventually settled in general practice.

As I was approaching my fortieth birthday, because of my eye problems, it became clear that I would not be able to work as a doctor for that much longer. In all honesty, this was far from the tragedy it could have been. I was starting to feel more and more frustrated with the limitations of my profession. The endless hours I was putting in caused a severe imbalance in my life. I spent most days treating diseases caused or worsened by stress. I felt more and more that I should be focusing on prevention of these diseases, rather than try and pick up the pieces once stress had damaged my patients physical and mental health.

I started looking at alternative options. I wanted to work fewer hours and focus on preventing stress from damaging my patients' health. I studied hypnosis and hypnotherapy. I qualified as a medical hypnotherapist at Birbeck College in London. I spent several years exploring alternative options, including NLP. I am a certified NLP practitioner.

Two years later I read a book that changed my life, the Tao of Equus by Linda Kohanov. It was written by Linda Kohanov. In this book, I discovered a promising new stress management strategy called equine-assisted psychotherapy.

You see, I had never forgotten that encounter in the meadow. I always yearned for a black horse of my own, but working full time as a doctor I just never had the time to make this happen.

Equine-assisted psychotherapy offered me the possibility of working with horses, while at the same time presenting me with an effective method of helping my patients reduce their stress levels. It also enabled me to work fewer hours. I would have time to spend with friends and family. I would be able to do this work with the sight I had left. This realisation convinced me that it was time take the plunge and change careers.

I had to make a lot of changes to re-balance my life. I had to say no, and mean it, many times. I resigned from my comfortable position as a general practitioner. I started studying equine-assisted psychotherapy and experiential learning through EAGALA (Equine-assisted growth and learning association). It was clear that my marriage of nearly 20 years was over, so I filed for divorce. When the divorce came through, married my current husband. I bought my first two horses. I sold my gorgeous farm in the Pays de la Loire in France. I moved to the United Kingdom, with my new husband and my two horses, leaving all my friends and family behind. Only to promptly move back to the south of France nine months and one very, very cold and wet winter later - husband, house, horses and all.

During this time of change, I thought a lot about balance. One thing I was sure of was that I still wanted to work preventing stress-induced and stress-related diseases, one way or another.

I had a good look at my strengths. I have had an excellent education. I had extensive experience (by then I had been in medical practice for nearly 20 years), especially in Psychiatry. I had a good look at my weaknesses and my limitations. Especially at my inability to work with the same intensity as I did before, in order to slow down the deterioration of my sight. I looked around me to see what opportunities I had. I found one hugely supportive husband, one magnificent Friesian mare, a drop-dead gorgeous Portuguese stallion and an overwhelming conviction that equine-assisted psychotherapy could be the most powerful agent for change in people's lives that I have ever encountered. We also were fortunate to have enough money to put down a deposit on a property. A farm that would house our growing equine family (the above-mentioned mare had managed to get herself pregnant by then) and us in a part of France we absolutely adored: Gascony, in the foothills of the majestic Pyrenees Mountains, on the border of France and Spain.

My husband and I had long discussions about how we could best use equine-assisted psychotherapy and experiential learning (he also trained with EAGALA, as an equine expert) to help people manage stress. We finally settled on running clinics and retreats. We wanted to host personal empowerment retreats and workshops. We realised that, like us, many of our friends yearned to live a more balanced, creative and meaningful life - a life more in alignment with their unique talents, values and ideals. No matter how much they desired to change the way they live, they were so busy trying to hold everything together that they ended up resigning themselves to their fate.

We wanted to offer our super-stressed friends somewhere to escape to from the challenges and demands of their daily lives. A place where they can relax and recharge their batteries. More than that, we wanted to equip them with the skills and tools they would need to create balance in their lives. We wanted to give them the tools they needed to manage stress once they returned home and so avoid the physical and mental harm prolonged stress could do to their health. We wanted to enable them to live the healthier, happier, more rewarding and more fulfilling lives that they deserved.

It took us a year to find the ideal property. Negotiating the sale took another 4 months. Finally, we owned a more than 200-year-old half-timbered Landaise farmhouse, partially renovated, with 20 acres of lush green pasture for the horses (crucially important). The house is idyllically located amongst vineyards, woods, orchards and meadows. The property came with a 2-acre fishing lake, fed by six constant springs and a small stream. We fell hook line and sinker for it the very first day we saw it. We had to fight tooth and nail to make it ours.

Why did we want it so badly? It is perfect for our needs. It is an ancient site of healing, possibly dating as far back as the Roman occupation of France. The six springs feeding the lake are reputed to have healing properties. For centuries, pilgrims on the St Jacques de Compostelle pilgrims' route have made a detour to the farm to drink the water from its springs and pray in its chapel. Apart from the original farmhouse, there is also a fully renovated barn, with ample accommodation for our family, friends, workshop and retreat guests.

After 15 months in livery, welcoming the horses to their new home was one of the happiest moments of my life. Our little herd had grown by then. We still had Belle de la Babinière, my stunningly beautiful Friesian mare. She now had competition in the beauty stakes from her daughter Aurore d'Alegria and from her half-sister, Tess des Sources Sacrées. Also in residence is Le Duc d'Alegria, Aurileo d'Alegria (our little rescue horse) and Baggio van't Kushti Grai, a drop-dead-gorgeous Tinker stallion.

Living here in the south of France has enabled us to create the balance we were looking for. Admittedly, we earn much less than we did in the past, but we also need so much less. We finally have time for what is important to us: each other, our health, our friends, our family, our church and our community. I very much suspect that living a balanced life is the secret to living a happy life.

If you would like to live a balanced life, I suggest you first take a step back and take a good look at what is important to you. It is useful to make a list of what matters to you most: your work, your significant other, your friends, your family, your health, your hobbies, your involvement in your community. Allocate a number from 1 to 10 to each of these, according to how satisfied you are with each category. How much time do you spend on each category? Do you spend most of your time working? We often do not even realise how unbalanced our lives are. To re-balance our lives, we may have to make some difficult decisions. I think it is important also to review this list at least once a year. It is important to adjust the time you spend on each category regularly.

If you would like to get an idea of how balanced your life is, have a look at the following questions:

Do you exercise regularly?

Do you eat a healthy, well-balanced diet?

Do you generally healthy?

Do you make time for prayer/meditation?

Do you limit the amount of pollution that you are exposed to; physically and mentally?

Do spend quality time every day with your significant other?

Do you allocate time to spend with your friends and family?

Do you contribute to the well-being of your community on a regular basis?

Do you have a clear career or business plan?

Are you satisfied with your income?

Do you enjoy your work?

Do you go on holiday and take all the days off that you are allowed?

Have you drawn up a budget and do you stay within its confines?

Do you have a savings or investment plan?

Do you give money to charity once a month?

Do you invest in your future by reading and learning new skills?

Do you make time to do whatever it is that you enjoy?

Do you invest in spiritual growth?

Do you celebrate your achievements?

If you can answer yes to most of these questions, your life is in balance. If not, then you may need to make some changes. If this exercise reveals that your life is unbalanced, one of the most useful things you can do to re-balance your life is to become more mindful. Mindfulness can help you become aware when you are behaving in a way that disturbs your equilibrium. I believe in mindfulness. It is not that I have anything against multi-tasking, not at all. Multi-tasking allows me to free up many precious minutes that I can spend on unbalanced areas in my life. Multi-tasking comes naturally to me; mindfulness does not. Or rather, it did not. I had to train myself to be mindful. To find out what mindfulness is all about, I watched a good number of excellent Ted talks on YouTube. I have gathered the ten best in a blog post. You read this blogpost at my website EquineGuidedGrowth.com just do a search for "Ten of the best Mindfulness Talks." Being mindful helps me balance my life minute-by-minute and so contributes directly to my happiness.

There is a lot of talking about mindfulness at the moment, about what it is and how it can benefit us. According to Jon Kabat-Zinn, the creator of the Mindfulness-Based Stress Reduction Method, mindfulness is "paying attention on purpose, in the present moment, and non-judgmentally, to the unfolding of experience moment to moment. Mindfulness means maintaining a moment-by-moment awareness of our thoughts, feelings, sensations and surroundings."

Why would anyone want to be more mindful? There are a variety of very good reasons. Mindfulness can

- reduce stress and so improve our mental and physical health,
- increase our productivity and our creativity,
- enhance our relationships by making couples more accepting of each other and also feel closer to one another,
- help us process our emotions more effectively and increase our emotional stability,

- improve our ability to concentrate, so that we can learn faster,
- reduce our vulnerability to pain,
- improve the quality of our sleep;
- improve our memory and
- slow down the ageing process.

I feel so serious about the benefits of mindfulness that I have written a whole book about the subject. Initially, the book was only meant as an accompaniment to my personal empowerment workshops, but as my knowledge and experience increased, so did the content of the book increase. Several of my workshop participants suggested that I make the book available to the general public. I eventually I published it as Mindfulness and Meditation in the south of France and later as Mindfulness and Meditation Options. The book introduces its readers to a variety of mindful meditation practises, like walking meditation, writing meditation, work meditation, music meditation etc. In an effort to help readers find a meditation practice that suits them and that they can incorporate seamlessly into their busy lives, without having to sacrifice too much of their precious time. It features a whole chapter about equine-guided mindfulness meditation, that, with equine-assisted experiential learning, forms the foundation of my workshops.

Mindfulness can help you notice when you are not managing your time efficiently. Good time management can enable us to live more balanced lives. French people, in general, have an interesting approach to time management. My French friends do not seem to get quite as stressed about their time constraints as I sometimes do. Arriving on time for dinner is not expected. In this part of France, arriving fifteen minutes late is the acceptable norm. No one expects you to arrive on time for a rendezvous. In the old days, I used to take a book to read should I have to wait for my friends to arrive at a restaurant. Now I have a tablet or mobile phone to amuse myself with.

I regretfully cannot claim that I am the world's best manager of time. When you have horses in your life, time becomes mobile rather than static. You learn the true meaning of the word 'flexible.' I have, however, had to pick up a couple of time management tricks to be able to look after our horses in the extravagant way that they have become accustomed to. Time management is not that difficult. You can manage time more efficiently while still remaining flexible. Before you jump in at the deep end, it is useful to understand how you currently spend your time. How much time do you spend working? How much time do you spend with your family and with your friends? How much time do you spend on yourself? The easiest way to figure this out is by keeping a time diary. I suggest you keep it for a week. The idea is to record how you spend your time. You may be surprised at how much time you spend surfing the net and checking your social media accounts. Nothing wrong with this, as long as it is in balance with the way you spend the rest of your time.

Once you know how you actually spend your time, you may want to make certain changes. You may notice that you spend most of your time working. Or you may notice that you spend all your free time watching television. The next step is to prioritise. I prioritise my tasks according to how urgent and how important they are. I got this idea from Stephan Covey. In his book, 7 Habits of Highly Effective People, he divides daily tasks into four groups. I have altered his method slightly. I divide my tasks into three groups:

- Important and urgent
- Not important but urgent
- Not urgent but important

I start every day with the important and urgent tasks. These tasks need to be done "tout de suite" (immediately). Today. If today is the last day I can pay the electricity bill before it gets cut off, it is an important and urgent task. I do not always do these tasks myself. I sometimes manage to overcome my perfectionism and delegate or outsource a task. It is always worthwhile keeping these two alternatives in mind. I do the not important but urgent tasks next. Doing these tasks today will avoid disastrous consequences in the near or not-so-near future. Next in line are the not urgent but important tasks. Like paying the water bill when it arrives instead of waiting until the last minute to pay it. It may not be urgent, but it will make my life easier in the long run. I have to keep an eye on myself with the tasks in this last group. If I don't, I procrastinate. I am very good at procrastinating! Despite all this careful planning, I still end up wasting time on tasks that are neither important nor urgent.

I make my lists in a notebook. I prefer this old-fashioned way to an app on my phone or a file on my computer. Even Evernote has not been able to seduce me. I find drawing a line through a task that I have completed more satisfying than deleting it. Whenever I think of something that needs to be done, I add it to one of the three groups. Sometimes I have to move tasks from one group to another, as they become more urgent. You can use sort of planning and scheduling tool: a pocket diary, a calendar, a wall chart, an app or a spreadsheet. Whatever suits you best.

Managing my time in this way helps me to keep things in perspective. It helps me allocate my time more efficiently. It provides a visual aid to help me decide if my life is in balance. When my life is balanced, I feel more confident that I will be able to handle unexpected emergencies. Despite my perfectionism, I think that asking for help, delegating and outsourcing are important aspects of successful time management. French women know this, and this is why they make time to create and nurture supportive relationships. In the next chapter, I talk to my friend Claire about support systems and how crucial support from friends and family is, especially as you get older.

Chapter 4

Rock-solid Support Systems

While I was writing this book, I sometimes got a bit de-motivated. I kept getting the all-this-has-been-said-before-I-don't-know-why-I-bother blues.

When it got really bad, I would take an afternoon off to go and walk the Camino de Santiago pilgrim's route. We are lucky; this centuries-old route passes a few kilometres east of our house. I started doing this after I saw an interview with Paulo Coelho on YouTube. If I remember correctly, he said he was inspired to write his book 'The Pilgrimage: A Contemporary Quest for Ancient Wisdom' while walking the Camino. Either way, walking the Camino inspired him to start writing.

I never paid much attention to the Camino before. I know that thousands of people walk the Camino ever year. I know that people have walked the Camino for the last 800 years. I know that most say that it had been a life-changing experience. I know that people from all walks of life walk it, whether they are religious or not. I know that several books have been written about it. One of my favourites is the actress Shirley MacClain's book – The Camino: A Spiritual Journey. I know that several films have been made about the Camino.

It is just that I have a lot to do, most days. I have the horses to look after. I have the vegetable garden, the flower garden, and the herb garden to maintain. I have to keep the paddocks clean. I have to take care of our retreat guests when they are here. I have to spend time with my husband, with our friends, and with our family. I barely have time to write. Never mind wasting an afternoon walking in the French countryside, however enticing it may be.

It isn't even as if I am a novice writer. This is not my first book. It is my second book. Several years ago, I wrote a book for horse riders who have fallen off their horses, who may have gotten injured and who are now too scared to get back on. Horse riders are like that. They always want to get back on their horses even if the idea scares them witless. My book, Horse Riding Confidence Secrets, does quite well for itself on Amazon, so I do have some confidence in my ability to write.

I also know that that there is a demand for books about self-confidence. I would say that 90% of the women who attend our clinics and retreats want one thing more than anything else. They want to feel more self-assured. They also want to be more assertive. They want to be able to say 'No' when they need to without feeling guilty. They do not want to have to explain why they are refusing. The horses are very good at helping our guests to be more assertive. Especially women who have never been anywhere near a horse or women who are scared of horses. Overcoming their fear of telling a one-ton stallion what to do increases their self-confidence, in a very practical and dramatic way.

When the fact that blog post after blog post has already been written about what women can do to increase their self-esteem weighs heavily on my mind, I spend an afternoon walking along 800-hundred-year-old paths through the wood. I walk through quaint medieval villages, lost-in-time, through sunflower fields, alongside rushing rivers and along sleeping lakes. Many of these blog posts are so well written that I wonder how anyone could possibly be interested in what I have to say. All this information is available for free. Why would anyone pay to buy a book about confidence building techniques when everything that needs to be said might already have been said?

It may be de-motivating, but I am not someone who gives up easily. Once I started writing, I knew I would have to finish the book. It was a question of finding ways to stay motivated to keep on writing. To overcome the occasional complete writer's block. So I walked the Camino. Once a week, when I could. Even though it was sometimes exhausting, it was always inspiring. So much so that it motivated me to create a residential "Walking and Wine Tasting Weekend Workshop" for writers with writer's block. Writers attending this workshop stay with us for three days and two nights. They have the opportunity to walk the Camino on Saturday and again on Sunday. They soon get their inspiration and motivation to write back. I am sure that walking the Camino motivates and inspires them to start writing again. Although the wine tasting we do along the way may also have something to do with it.

On my walks, I met people. I met women. Amazing women, who are walking the Camino on their own, sometimes for weeks on end. I asked them about courage, and I asked them about confidence. Young women. Old women, sometimes way into their seventies. Every day they walk 15-20 km (10-15 miles). They sleep in dormitories and eat whatever they can grab on their way. They carry everything they need in a rucksack on their backs. Brave, independent women, of various nationalities walk the Camino.

It was on one of these walks that I met Claire. She taught me a few things about sustaining self-confidence that I never knew. Fancy that, there I was thinking I know everything there is to know about the subject. How wrong I was.

Claire is a seventy-seven-year old French woman. Fit as a fiddle, with a smile on her face and a knowing twinkle in her eye. She has had one hip replacement and two knee replacements. She walks the Camino every year, for a week to ten days, depending on her health. She prefers to walk in September, when the days are still long enough, but cooler than in August. Compared to other walkers, she carries a relatively small backpack. While walking, she makes ample use of her two Nordic walking sticks.

When I came up to her, I naturally could not resist that smile. I fell into pace next to her, to see if she wanted to talk while we walked together. The Camino has its own etiquette. One does not just start talking to other walkers. Some people want to walk on their own. They want to think their thoughts in peace and quiet. Some are meditating while they are walking. It would be very impolite to interrupt.

No such reluctance with Claire, she was very happy to chat. She even thought it might be a good idea to sit down on that fallen tree trunk to have a drink. She told me that she came from Normandy, land the blond-and-blue-eyed Viking descendants. Her hair still retained a blond hue. Even though it was windswept now, it was clearly well-kept and well-cut. Her laughing blue eyes were sparkling like a young girl's. I know Normandy fairly well. I owned a farm there for 12 years while I worked in the Channel Islands, so we had many memories to share.

Eventually, I asked her what I ask all French women whom I meet while walking the Camino: Where does she get the courage and confidence from to walk this challenging route all on her own?

"Well, I always loved walking. I always loved walking on my own. Walking the Camino for the first time did not seem as much of a challenge as it should have seemed. You have to remember; I was much younger then. I never realised how difficult it was going to be! Not so much physically, really, but mentally. Walking 800 kilometres on your own is tough. Yes, indeed. The first time I walked the Camino, I did so from beginning to end. On my own. I learnt a lot of things about myself and about other people. I had lots of time to think, about all sorts of things. Mostly about what a crazy idea it had been to decide to walk the Camino! I met lots of people: couples, families, small groups, men on their own and rarely, another woman on her own. Most were busy with their own thoughts during the day, but eager to share their experiences over dinner. I learnt so much. I learnt the value of encouragement and support from other people.

Were the French women I met more resilient than other women? Maybe. Yes, maybe they were. I noticed it, especially among the solo walkers. I think it might be because French women carry elaborate support systems with them, at all times. Years ago, it was more difficult to access these systems. You could use the phone in villages you walked through. You could write letters home and pick up waiting letters in villages where your family knew you were going to sleep over. You could send and receive telegrams. Now things are much easier, of course. Now the average Frenchwoman's support system really comes into its own, with the advent of mobile phones and computers. Maybe French women are more confident because they have extensive support systems to back them up?

As you know, French women start building life-long friendships at a very early age. We are encouraged to make friends in nursery school. We are encouraged to solidify these friendships in elementary school. We are taught how to nurture these friendships. By the time you get to my age, you have friends, men and women, who have been part of your life for these last seventy-four years. Of course, we make new friends during our lifetimes. They are important too, but it is these seven-decades-long friendships that give me the most confidence. Knowing that I have friends who love me despite everything I did or didn't do. Loyal friends, who have stood by me through thick and thin, who accept me just as I am...they give me courage. And confidence, of course. I think it is because we benefit from this sort of friendships that we are more confident maybe then women who were not encouraged to make lifelong friends from an early age.

Also, the emphasis French people put on the importance of family makes a difference. Especially as you get older. My mother taught me to respect my family: my grand-parents, my uncles, my aunts, my great-uncles and my great-aunts. My cousins and I spend a lot of time together as children and maintained that contact during adulthood, so that my children grew up surrounded by their own cousins, aunts, uncles and grand-parents. Now that there are few of those left, I enjoy the rejuvenating company of my children, my grand-children, my nieces and my nephews. It is not always plain sailing. We French are an emotional lot. We frequently fall out, but we always make up again. Blood is, after all, thicker than water. Even if it does sometimes take a decade or two. I digress. What I mean to say is that having the support of a family that size behind you makes you feel confident. Now in my old age, the respect – no, never mind that – the interest that my grand-children show in what I get up to makes me so happy, I feel as if my heart would burst. I am lucky, also, that my two best friends from the Maternelle come from as healthy and as long-living stock as I do. They are enthusiastic in their support of my mad-cap adventures. I had hoped my friend Lise would join me on this year's walk, but she recently met some old Frenchman. She is head-over-heels in love. No chance of separating the two lovebirds, not even for a week.

Having lived in the same Norman village all my life, the same village and house my parents and grandparents lived in, also make a difference. I have always been part of the community. I was "conseillière" for more than thirty years, on and off. I was involved with everything that went on in our village. My daughter now lives in the old family farmhouse. I have moved into a "cozee" (the French pronunciation of cosy) little house in the heart of the village. I love village life. I love playing cards with my contemporaries, especially during the winter. We are very competitive. Us lot also look after "les anciens", you know, the old people. We organise thé-dansants on Sunday afternoons for the old folk. My community knows me. The people from my village value my input, they respect me. Makes me feel confident, I can tell you. Of course, I also go to Mass, fairly regularly. Our village no longer has a priest. We go to the closest town for Mass. Some of us have been attending Mass together for as long as we can remember. We have supported each other through many difficult times. Knowing that these people are there for me when I need them makes me feel that I can do anything, I set my mind to.

Now we have the internet. We can stay in contact at all times. In my old age, I have made new friends. Some of these friends I met while walking the Camino. They have now gone back to their own countries but are still in contact on Facebook. Every year, when I walk the Camino, they follow my progress day by day. I put a post on Facebook every evening. I add a picture or two. It makes them feel as if they are walking the Camino with me. They encourage me when I feel tired. They tease me when I blame the tiredness on my aching bones. Sometimes they text me during the day with words of encouragement. I have to mute my phone to be able to pay attention to my own thoughts! The fact that they are interested at all makes me feel good. I nurture these friendships with as much ardour as I nurtured my Maternelle friendships. There is more to it than that, though. It also makes me feel safe. I am no longer a spring chicken. You may have noticed (I fervently shook my head, as expected). If something should happen to me, I can phone the pompiers. They will know exactly where I am because they can locate my phone with GPS. You can't even get lost on the Camino anymore. Knowing that my friends and family know exactly where I am and that help can be summoned with a single phone call, fills me with confidence.

In my opinion, French women's penchant for creating trustworthy support systems for themselves has a lot to do with their healthy self-esteem.

I tend to agree with Claire. I would add that French women are privileged to have strong role models: in history, in politics, in commerce, in everyday life. I would go as far as to say that a French women's value is judged less by her beauty and youth than by her achievements and expertise. Advancing age seems to have less of a detrimental influence on a woman's value in France than it does elsewhere. This seems to ring true even for actresses. Take one example: Catherine Deneuve. One of the best-loved French actresses. At 72 she is as popular as she was in her youth, probably even more so. Her beauty is as celebrated now in her seventies as it was in her twenties and thirties. Role models are important. French women can find inspiration from a large variety of strong, intelligent, confident, successful and beautiful women of all ages. They can model themselves on their favourite role models. Mentors are important too. A mentor is similar to a role model, I think, just more accessible. Someone you respect. Someone you can talk to, someone who listens and helps you with your problems.

One of my mentors was my father's sister, Angela. Sadly, she died a few months ago. I have decided not to mourn her death, but to celebrate her life: everything that she had achieved, all the people's lives that she had enriched, the wonderful moments we have shared... her generosity, her quick understanding, her sharp intellect, her lasting beauty, her determination, her perseverance, her inner strength, her unfailing support, her enduring sense of humour, her cutting wit, her strong Christian beliefs, her ingenuity, her creativity, her humanity, her humility and her gentle smile.

My aunt Angela taught me that anything is possible, that I can do anything I set my mind to and that patience and perseverance are always rewarded. Of course, she was not perfect, she had her faults, just as I have mine. We disagreed about many things. She did, after all, teach me to make up my own mind about things. She taught me that when I have made it up, to speak my mind without reservation. We also had a lot in common. Sometimes understanding would pass between us in a single glance.

I will never forget her. I feel profoundly grateful to have known her.

What can you, who may not have spent your childhood making friends and nurturing friendships, do to increase your self-confidence? I think it is never too late to build an extensive support system. Making friends is not that difficult, nurturing relationships is a little more complicated. It needs work. I think it was Ralph Waldo Emerson who said: "The only way to have a friend is to be one." If you want to make a friend and nurture your relationship, you are first going to have to be a good friend.

To be a good friend, you need to

- Be your own best friend first. If you cannot accept and appreciate yourself as you are, you won't be able to accept and appreciate others. If you cannot forgive yourself for past mistakes, you won't be able to forgive friends' mistakes. A friend is someone who understands your past, believes in your future and accepts you just the way you are. That is the sort of friend you want to be to yourself.
- Be yourself. Do not try to be someone you are not in the hope that people will like you. Do not try to be the person you think your friend expects you to be.
- Make time to get to know your new friend. What do you have in common? About what do you disagree? What do you both like/dislike? Find common ground. Trust is best based on knowledge. Trust is the foundation of friendship. If you trust, you will be trusted.
- Listen with your heart and with your mind. Do not just listen to reply. Just listen. Hear what is not being said. Be comfortable with the occasional silence. Wait before you reply. Make sure you understand what your friend is trying to say. Listen long and listen hard. Do not give advice unless solicited. If you do, spare each other's feelings.
- Take a genuine interest in each other's lives. As Dale Carnegie said, "You can make more friends in two months by becoming interested in other people than you can in two years by trying to get people interested in you."
- Commit to the friendship. This means being there for each other at all times, middle of the night, middle of a meeting, middle of a holiday. Make time for each other. Check up on each other. Keep in touch. It can be difficult to create times to get together, so take advantage of common activities and interests you have.

- Share your hopes, your dreams, your failures, your disappointments. Share your victories, big or small. Celebrate together. Learn from each other's experiences.
- Support each other. Support your friend even if you cannot support her behaviour or her opinion. It is OK to say," I don't agree." You can still be supportive. Don't give up on a friend because he/she made the wrong choice or isn't the person you want them to be. Appreciate and accept your friends as they are, unconditionally.
- Help each other grow. Encourage each other. Go on workshops together. Read personal growth books together. Help each other back on the road less travelled if one goes astray.
- It is OK to disagree. Just agree to disagree. Don't obsess about small disagreements. Forgive. Forget. Apologise first. Do not hold grudges.
- Be loyal. If you give your word, keep it. Tell your friend, "I have got your back," and mean it. Be dependable, keep your promises. Be trustworthy.
- Be understanding. Put yourself in your friend's shoes. Imagine what he/she is feeling (when you are together but also when you are not together). See the problem from your friend's perspective, before you show it to him/her from your perspective.
- Do not manipulate your friends, not even for their own good. Only make use of your friends by being of use to them.
- Be generous. Be grateful for their friendship and tell them that you are. Send a card. Buy flowers/a small gift. Any friendship worth maintaining needs nurturing. Give as much to the relationship as you get from it. A good friendship is based on respect, balance and equality.
- Cheer each other up. Most people, when asked, say they want a friend they can laugh with. Always give humour free access to your friendship. Make each other laugh.
- Know when to let go and walk away without making excuses.

Having this sort of friend's support is a tremendous boost to one's self-confidence. Even if she has not known you all her life, her support can still be invaluable. Maybe you have lost contact with your childhood friends, your siblings or your cousins. Maybe you have grown apart. You can look them up again if you want. It is easier than ever now. Just do a quick search on Facebook. Or access one of those websites that re-unite long lost friends and family. Re-igniting an abandoned friendship doesn't always work, but it is always worth a try.

These days, we can find support easily. The internet allows us to connect with women all over the world. Some people say an "internet friendship" is not a real friendship. I am not so sure – maybe it is not as intense, but the support is as real. While I was writing this book, I got loads of support from the members of a Facebook group that I joined earlier this year. The group is called BlogShareLove. There are only 28 of us in the group, sometimes less. We have been supporting each other's' blogging efforts for months. We have gotten to know each other well. The support of these women, who know exactly how well I can or cannot write, many who write much better than I do, mean the world to me. Sometimes one finds role models and mentors in the most unexpected places!

When you are building your confidence-boosting support system, don't forget about the internet. Virtual friends can be as supportive and confidence-building as real-life friends can. You can also find role models on-line, as well as mentors and coaches.

Blogging itself did a lot to boost my self-confidence. Not so much in the beginning, but more so as time went by. Blogging requires work, and with that, I do not mean writing blog posts. You can create a phenomenal blog, but if you do not promote your blog posts, no one is going to read them. I took up blogging because living here in peaceful, blissful, deepest rural France in the winter can make me feel a bit lonely. Yes, I have a wonderful husband, and I have the horses. I have some loved-to-bits friends, and I stay in contact with my friends and family further afield on Facebook. Just sometimes I miss being a doctor, even if it is only for the daily interaction. Being a female general practitioner meant that most of my patients were women. I miss sharing their lives. I often saw around 30 – 40 patients a day, so I sometimes feel a bit isolated here in one of the least-populated departments of France. I enjoy being a member of a couple of groups here, the LLC (Ladies Lunch Club) de l'Armagnac, to name one. Members meet once a month for lunch at a local restaurant. There are 100+ members, and at least 40 show up every month for lunch. I also sing in a choir or two. We meet once a week. Although I very much appreciate the friends that I have here, I miss talking to women in person, from all walks of life and of all ages, on a daily basis.

I finally decided that life is too short to expect new friends to come looking for me. I was going to have to go out there and find them myself, so I decided to try blogging. I soon realised that I would have to make an effort to get my carefully crafted blog posts read. It was clear that I was going to have to do some serious studying. Arrrrgh...just the thought of studying makes me come out in spots. When I retired from medicine, I thought I had finished with formal education. Once I started studying, it was quite clear that I did not know anything much about how to promote blog posts at all.

When I first stepped into the blogosphere, I could not make head or tail of all the new terminology. Linky parties? Follow to Follow? Blog Love? Throwback Thursday? Sharing on Twitter, Facebook, Pinterest? I did think Pinterest was great because I used it to collect interior decorating pictures. I love French Country Style. I created my Pinterest identity, Margaretha's Muse, solely so that I could have somewhere to store my French Country Style Pinterest pictures. These come in very helpful when I decorate our house. Round here, I am a Pinterest pioneer. Most of my friends here have never even heard of Pinterest. Now I have all sorts or Pinterest boards. I have a Confident Women board, an Equine-assisted Experiential Learning board, a Mindfulness and Meditation board, a Gascony board (our region in France), a Self-Confidence and Self-esteem board, a Support System board...at last count I had twenty-seven. When I first read articles about "How to create re-pinnable pins" and "How to use Pinterest to increase traffic to your blog" though, I was flummoxed. I thought Twitter is a waste of time. Who can manage to say anything useful in 140 characters? Only one of my friends had ever heard of Twitter, and that is because she is a website designer. I can barely believe it myself, but my Twitter account Margaretha Montagu (@equineguidedMD) now has more than 12 000 followers.

The difference between Facebook pages and Facebook profiles? I did not have a clue. Today my Margaretha Montagu Facebook page has more than two thousand likes and my Empowering Women Facebook page is catching up quickly. Finally, my blog posts are being read.

To get my blog posts read, I had to make new friends. On Pinterest, on Facebook, and on Twitter. I had to identify new role models. Find new mentors. I made friends and I work hard to sustain these new relationships. I found a mentor and learnt a lot. Successful blogging role models are in no short supply. The more blogging friends I made, the more support I had and the more confident I became about blogging. I think I also wrote better posts. More and more of my posts were being read and commented on. Blogging really can be a great confidence-generator, as long as you are willing to build your support system by supporting other bloggers.

Wasn't it Socrates who said, "Be slow to fall into friendship; but when thou art in, continue firm and constant"?

Making virtual friends is satisfying, but making real friends is even more rewarding. The women I met and the friends I have made during our workshops have enriched my life in many different ways. Most women who attend our workshops make friends here. They stay in contact with each other in the years that follow. They sometimes arrange to meet up at a workshop a year or two later. Seeing our guests make friends with each other and with the horses is probably one of the most gratifying parts of hosting these workshops. There are a couple of other things that I appreciate about hosting these workshops. You can find out more here: My 13 favourite things about hosting workshops in France.

In the next chapter, you will meet a nun, Sister Marie-Therèse. Fasten your seatbelt.

Chapter 5

Gratitude and Generosity

I suspect that French women are confident because they know how much they have to be grateful for. When I was a newly-qualified doctor, I met a young nun in the hospital where I was working. At the time, Sister Marie-Therèse was not much older than I was. Her parents were from the Ivory Coast. They had emigrated to France before Marie-Therèse was born. She grew up in one of the suburbs of Paris. She described her childhood as a happy one. Her parents both worked full-time. Marie-Therèse did well at school, and her parents were proud of her. When she decided at the age of 11 that she wanted to become a nun, her devout Roman Catholic parents did not object. Her father insisted that she first attend a lycée so that she can learn more about the trials, tribulations and temptations people have to face. After getting her bac, Marie-Therèse joined a convent. After her confirmation, she had an opportunity to go to Africa to work in a hospital there for a few months. Marie-Therèse was appalled at the lack of basic medical care in the more remote villages. She felt called to go and help the people there. Her Mother Superior suggested that she work for a few months at a hospital here in France before she leaves, to get some nursing experience.

As we had Africa in common (I did my medical training there), we were soon firm friends. Many a cold winter's night we warmed each other with memories of endless warm and sunny African days. Marie-Therèse intrigued me. Here was a beautiful young woman. She exuded calm and confidence while I was feeling insecure, acutely aware of my inexperience as a medical doctor. I asked her what made her feel so confident, so able to handle whatever stressful situation came her way.

"If I am confident, it is because I know that I am unconditionally loved. By God."

"I know that and I understand that," I answered, "but is that all there is to it? Don't you ever feel insecure?"

"Of course," she quipped, "I am only human after all. When I feel worry gnawing at my confidence, I make a list of all the things I that I am good at. I feel deeply grateful for the talents God has equipped me with to do His work. Making a list of what I am good at, boosts my confidence significantly."

I learnt a lot about the relationship between confidence and gratitude from Sister Marie-Thérèse.

One evening, after we had finished our work for the day., sister Marie-Thérèse smiled her sweet smile at me. She said, "There is something I want to ask you. I seem to get every single cold that comes onto the ward. It seems as if it is getting more and more difficult to get rid of each subsequent one." Having been taught that the most obvious diagnosis is often the right one, I asked about her eating habits. I wanted to find out if she may have a vitamin deficiency that reduced her resistance against colds. She was eating healthily and taking good care of herself, so I soon put that diagnosis out of my mind. I did a quick physical examination, that did not shed any light on the subject. I had noticed that she had lost a bit of weight lately. On her tall, slender frame this was quickly noticeable. We had been working hard, trying to cope with the annual winter flu epidemic, so I had assumed this was the cause for her weight loss. I suggested a few blood tests, just to make sure. I pulled out a few forms and as I started filling them in, a nasty suspicion formed in my mind. I immediately rejected it, it was quite impossible. I couldn't let it go, though. I found myself pulling a form up that we rarely used in those days.

"Sister, there is another blood test that I would like to do, but I need your written consent to it. It is extremely unlikely, but I think we need to do this test to put our minds at rest."

Marie-Thérèse looked down at the form. "HIV? You think I may have AIDS? But how could that even be possible? I have never even slept with a man!"

I tried to reassure her that it was unlikely. I asked if she had ever pricked herself with a needle while she was in Africa. She said she could not remember. She thought she hadn't. We talked about other possible causes. I was ready to let it go when she changed her mind and agreed to take the test. "Maybe it is not such a bad idea, after all. If I do have it, I would not want to put any of my patients at risk."

Against all expectations, the test came back positive. We started treatment immediately. Marie-Therèse fought like a lioness for months, but it was a particularly virulent strain. It finally became clear that she was never going to make it back to Africa. I spent the last weeks of her life with her. It was during this time that she taught me what being grateful for what you have truly meant.

Sister Marie-Therèse spent her last days on earth counting her blessings. I still treasure her friendship today, nearly two decades after her death. Her confidence never wavered. When I fell my confidence sagging, I make a list of my friends. I am grateful for each and every one and I am grateful that I have a long list. The length and quality of this list fill me with confidence. How can I not feel confident that so many people care about me despite my even longer lists of weaknesses?

I am grateful for my four-legged friends as much as I am for my two-legged friends.

I am grateful for the friends who sing in choirs with me and the friends who go I to church with me. I am grateful for my school friends and for my university friends. I am grateful for the Facebook groups I belong to and for the friends I have made there. Friends who regularly offer support and understanding. I am grateful for old and new friends, for young and older friends and for busy friends who still find time for me.

I am grateful for friends who send me parcels, for friends who buy me small gifts and for friends who remember my birthday. I am grateful for family members who are also friends. I am grateful for friends who share my interests - my horsey friends who understand before I had time to put my thoughts into words, my music friends who are moved to tears by the same music I am, my Christian friends who pray with me. I am grateful for friends who have the same occupation as I do and understand the demands and challenges I face. I am grateful for friends from different cultures who have enriched my life and have broadened my horizons.

My friends are my world, no matter where in the world they find themselves. They are always in my thoughts.

Ralph Waldo Emerson said, "The glory of friendship is not the outstretched hand, nor the kindly smile, nor the joy of companionship; it is the spiritual inspiration that comes to one when he discovers that someone else believes in him and is willing to trust him." My friends listen to me. They allow me to rant and to rave and to work through my anger or disappointment. They point out opportunities to me, and they celebrate my successes with me. They encourage me when I have eye problems. They buy me flowers, make me jam from the fruit in their gardens and invite me to dinner to cheer me up when I am low. They buy me inspiring books. They look after my animals when I go away. They send me cheerful messages on Facebook... I cannot imagine my life without them.

My friends help me when I make mistakes. This happens often. They help me when I misunderstand which is not difficult considering I spend less than 1% of my time speaking my mother tongue. They chide me when I have wronged someone, when I have forgotten a kindness or when I have neglected to return a favour, bless them. I am so grateful that despite my flaws, even when I knowingly or unknowingly offend them, they are always prepared to forgive.

Having friends like these fills me with confidence.

I am grateful for the handful of friends who are close enough to me to have walked with me through the valley of blindness, never tiring, never despairing, never judging, never complaining.

The best kind of friend is the one you could sit next to on a bench, never say a word to and walk away feeling like that was the best conversation you have ever had. I am so lucky to have found so many friends who know the value of silence, none more so than our horses. Belle will always be my closest horse-friend, my soul-mare. We have shared more than I have shared with any of our other horses. Belle's daughter Aurore is a good friend too, if somewhat temperamental in her affections. So is Duc. He has often offered a shoulder for me to cry on, even when he does not fully understand what the problem is. Whenever he sees me, he whinnies a greeting and comes trotting up to me, even from the furthest corner of his paddock. Not to forget my canine and feline friends, especially our Belgian Shephard Melchi'ore, who sticks to my side like glue when she suspects something might be wrong.

Marie-Therèse also thought me that gratitude without action is worthless. Gratitude should blossom into generosity. Generosity could simply mean that you thank your friends for their loyalty today. Tomorrow may be too late.

Thank them for telling you the truth. For talking things through with you. For meeting you halfway. For being compassionate. For thinking of you often, for making time for you. For giving you their full attention when you are talking. For appreciating you as you are. For knowing when something is wrong. For making the extra effort to understand you. For supporting your decisions and for being there through good times and bad. Thank them for believing in you. Thank them for being patient, forgiving, understanding, supportive and encouraging.

Isn't it remarkable how often confident women are also generous women? The French women I am lucky enough to have as friends are generous women. Since we have moved to the French countryside, I have come across this confident generosity more often than ever before. Is this a characteristic of the women of the Gers, more so than of other regions? I do not know. All I know is that I have never met with as much ready generosity as I have since we live here.

I have made several new friends since we bought our farm here. My new friends are confident women who have lived here for most of their lives. They have generously shared their local knowledge, their time and their expertise. Amongst these supremely confident and generous women, one stands out head-and-shoulders above the others: my friend Lisa. Lisa has been teaching me about confidence and generosity for the last six years. She instructs me, not by telling me how to go about it, but by setting an example. I have lost count of the times she has come to my aid, the times she has stood by me, the times she has encouraged me to keep going.

When we first moved to her village, Lisa made sure that we got involved with the local community. We were soon taking part in the annual New Year's pageant. I couldn't act, and my husband couldn't speak French, but that did not seem to matter. She graciously introduced us to the other villagers. She ensured that we were invited to various village events. She invited me to join the choir she was singing in and in which I sang until its demise a year ago. Whenever we needed something for our farm, she immediately knew who to contact for help. When we needed hay for the winter, to feed the horses, she asked around until she found a young farmer who could supply us. She negotiated a price that she thought was reasonable, much less than we were willing to pay. When we needed a plumber, she pointed us in the right direction. When we needed an electrician, she knew just the chap. When I needed fresh fruit for our workshop guests, Lisa provided. When we needed to go away, she looked after the horses until we came back. When we needed somewhere to store our furniture, she asked around in the village until she found an empty house where we could store our belongings. For fifteen months.

Meeting someone as generous as Lisa once in a lifetime might not be that exceptional, but Lisa was not the only woman in our village who helped us. None of these people are particularly wealthy. Sometimes just the opposite, but they always had time to listen to a problem, offer a good word of advice or lend a piece of equipment.

Did you know that being grateful is not just good for your self-esteem, it can also be beneficial to your physical, mental and spiritual health? Studies have proved (see Dr. Robert Emmons' book, Thanks! How practising Gratitude can make you Happier, that gratitude can strengthen your immune system and make you less bothered by aches and pains. It can motivate you to exercise more and to take better care of yourself. It can make you sleep longer and feel more refreshed upon waking. It can also make you more positive, alert, alive, awake, joyful, optimistic and happy. Gratitude can make you more helpful, generous, compassionate, forgiving, outgoing and appreciative. So why not express your gratitude by paying it forward with a few random acts of kindness?

Random acts of kindness come in many shapes and forms. It can be something as simple as offering a smile to a passer-by. Or paying a well-deserved compliment.

You could…

- leave your newspaper behind in the coffee shop for someone else to read,
- put 50 pence into a nearly empty parking meter,
- help a mother with her pushchair up or down the stairs,
- post an encouraging comment on Facebook,
- let the person behind you in the queue pay first if they have only one or two items,
- give someone a book you think they would like,
- stop to talk to a homeless person,
- pay the toll for the car behind you,
- hold the elevator,
- send a supportive text message
- give up your seat to someone on a crowded bus,
- donate your old clothes to a charity,
- shop for someone who is ill,
- donate your used books to your local library,
- help someone who is struggling with heavy bags or
- give someone the benefit of the doubt.

People are more prepared to do commit random acts of kindness than one might realise. Last year I wrote a Christmas post for my blog entitled Random Acts of Kindness Advent Calendar. It was the first of my blog posts ever to go viral. I feel so serious about the benefits that expressing your gratitude may have that I wrote a book about it. The book is called Mindfully navigating Change with Gratitude and Generosity - at any Age! It includes a gratitude and generosity journal, because keeping a Gratitude and Generosity Journal can help you facilitate change as follows:

- Gratitude journaling can make you more creative, thus enhancing your problem-solving skills and making it easier to cope with the difficulties that making changes can create.
- When you take the time to focus on the good things in your life, those things that you feel grateful for, big and small, you

are focusing on the positive aspects of your life, instead of on the negative. This can help you become more positive in general. To make changes effectively, you need to remain positive even when things go wrong, as they will.
- As you instigate change, as YOU change, gratitude journaling can give you a new perspective on what is important to you now and what you truly appreciate in your new life. Journaling helps you decide what you want to have more of in your life, and what you can do without. It helps you determine what really matters to you.
- Keeping a gratitude journal helps become more self-aware. It gives you the opportunity to acknowledge and be grateful for your achievements. Because you are celebrating your own success, you are less likely to compare yourself with others and resent their success. It thus increases your self-esteem as well as your self-confidence.
- Gratitude journaling can help you sleep better. When you are making changes, it is easy to get into the habit of worrying at night. Spending just 15 minutes before you fall asleep writing down what you felt grateful about that day, can help you get a much better night's sleep. By reminding yourself of what you have to be thankful for, you are much less likely to worry and therefore you will sleep much better.
- Gratitude and generosity journaling can improve your both you physical and psychological health. People who express their gratitude feel generally happier and healthier than people who do not. They care better for themselves, get more regular exercise, and arrange more frequent check-ups with their doctor than those who don't. Gratitude journaling will inspire you to look after your physical and mental health, which will make you will be more resilient and enable you to cope with stress better, especially the stress generated from making changes.
- On difficult days, on days that you feel you will never be able to change, you can read through your gratitude and generosity journal and discover how much you have changed already.
- I firmly believe that expressing your gratitude in this way, especially if it spills over into an act of generosity, attracts

even more things to be grateful for. Generosity isn't always about money, it can also be about kindness, compassion, empathy, acknowledgement and acceptance.
- Gratitude and Generosity journaling can instil a sense of connectedness – to ourselves, to others, to nature, to our community, to our hopes and dreams for ourselves, for those we care about and for our planet.
- If generosity is a characteristic of a confident woman, a generous woman no doubt feels more confident when she helps others.

The fake-it-till-you-make-it approach is not one I believe in without reserve. Although there may be something to it, if you are trying to increase your self-esteem. Even if you are not 100% confident yet, you can start being grateful and generous right away. Someone's reaction to your generosity might be confidence-boosting in its own right. People are not always grateful. Some people can be downright ungrateful, no matter what you do for them. Doing something for someone else, even if they do not acknowledge your generosity, can still make you feel good about yourself, especially if you are generous without expecting anything in return. Lisa taught me this, she never expects anything in return. For Lisa, the pleasure is in the giving.

Giving is not always easy. I know that from personal experience. When I develop new, unexpected eye problems that put my sight at risk, my confidence dropped right through the soles of my riding boots. With a thud. It is difficult to feel generous and to help other people when you can barely handle your own problems. Once, I needed three major operations in quick succession. Lisa stood by me, as always. I decided that I wanted to go and thank her in person, for all the help that she was giving us in so many little and so many big ways. It was a good thing we went to see them because we found out that Lisa's husband was about to have an emergency operation himself for a potentially life-threatening condition. She did not mention it to me as she did not want me to worry. Supporting her through this trial helped me to stop obsessing about my own problems. It put my problems into perspective and helped me cope with them more efficiently. Doing something for someone else took my mind off my own problems and it made me feel more confident about handling them.

Gratitude can help you to change your focus. This can be a good thing. When you are stressed, you may be focusing either on the future or on the past. If you focus on the past you may be thinking:

- How could everything have gone so terribly wrong?
- Why did that this have to happen to me now?
- Did I do the right thing? Or did I get everything completely wrong?
- I wish I can go back and do things differently!

When you are focusing on the future, you may be thinking:

- What are other people going to think and say about me?
- What if something goes seriously wrong?
- Will I be able to handle the situation?
- What if I make a complete idiot of myself?

Gratitude anchors you in the immediate present. It helps you to focus on what you have to be thankful for right now. You can still plan for the future. You can still learn from the past, but you are less likely to dwell on it. When you are stressed, about either the future or the past, your body remains in constant "fight or flight" mode. In this state of emergency, your immune system is challenged, your sleep pattern is disrupted, and you become irritable, angry and unable to concentrate. When you focus your attention on what you are grateful for now, your entire body relaxes. You feel more confident and less stressed. According to Wikipedia, "grateful people are happier, less depressed, less stressed and more satisfied with their lives and social relationships."

After the incident with Lisa's husband, I asked several of my confident French friends how they remained mindful of being grateful in stressful situations. It seemed that keeping a gratitude diary is a very useful way of training oneself to be grateful. All you have to do is to write down three things a day, or even once a week, that you are grateful for. Writing this down has advantages over just thinking it. It involves more than one of our senses, and so deepens the emotional impact.

Using a gratitude journal makes sense to me. It is a tangible, visible and tactile reminder. It has dated pages that make it immediately obvious if I missed a day. It means I can look back a week, a month or a year later and remind myself of all the things I had to be thankful for in the past. Even if I did miss a day here and there. It helped me to establish the habit of paying attention to gratitude-inspiring events. I do not think it is essential to write something every single day. It is more important to go for quality rather than quantity.

With "quality" I mean that you should not make a list in a rush just so that you can tick this chore off your daily to-do list. I reflect on each item on the list. I may add a few details. I think listing people to whom I am grateful has more of an impact than listing things for which I am grateful. I often use this prompt: "I am grateful for ...., because ...." A journal can be a notebook or a file on your computer. It can be a mason jar with pieces of paper in it, a scrapbook, an app on your phone, a Facebook page, a blog or a Pinterest board...whatever works for you. There are even websites that function as gratitude journals, like 365grateful.com. Or you could join the Gratitude Project by using the Thnx4.org website. Thnx4.org provides a guided two-week exercise designed by experts to make gratitude a daily practice. Participants keep a private journal and say "thanx" publicly through Facebook, Twitter or by email. In the end, they find out how 14 days of gratitude awareness affected their mood and health. By joining Thnx4.org, you will also be paying it forward as you will be helping scientists research data that will be used to study the causes, effects and meaning of gratitude. Using Thnx4.org will not only be hugely beneficial to you, but you will advance the research being done on gratitude, helping to answer questions such as:

-Do men tend to feel grateful for different things than women?
-Does gratitude practice have any discernible racial, ethnic or regional variations?
-Does there tend to be an ebb and flow of gratitude over our lifetimes?

I read quite a bit about the effect that being grateful can have on happiness, confidence and health. What really brings the concept home to me is our horses' reaction to gratitude. Especially our little rescue horse, Aurileo d'Alegria, or Leo to his friends. He was very badly abused before he came to us. He seems to find it difficult to believe that anyone would feel grateful towards him. It is probably not a human attitude that he has encountered too frequently in the past. He is noticeably calmer, more willing to be approached, even to be touched when I approach him with gratitude in my heart. I sometimes get the impression that he is trying to show me that he is grateful in return. Our other horses express their gratitude much more clearly. I am invariably greeted by a chorus of welcoming whinnies when I walk over to their paddock.

"True happiness is to enjoy the present, without anxious dependence upon the future, not to amuse ourselves with either hopes or fears but to rest satisfied with what we have, which is sufficient, for he that is so wants nothing. The greatest blessings of mankind are within us and within our reach. A wise man is content with his lot, whatever it may be, without wishing for what he has not." Seneca

In the next chapter, we take a light-hearted look at my friend Amelie's stress management strategies.

Chapter 6

Taming and Harnessing Stress

Have you ever wondered how they do it? How do French women stay so cool, calm and perfectly collected even in the most stressful situations? Anais must have been nervous during that fashion show. It must have crossed her mind, more than once, that something might go wrong. So how did she handle the stress? How did cope with that humiliating incident on the catwalk with such pizazz?

Millions of words have been written and published about stress: about the meaning of stress, about the symptoms of stress, about the causes of stress and about stress management. I have written a few thousand of those words myself. I think most of us by now have a good idea of what stress is, even if we are still not quite clear about what we can do about it. I have worked with patients suffering from stress for many years. I have suffered from stress-related illness myself. I have a very good idea of what stress is and of the damage it can do.

Stress is the body's reaction to any challenge that requires a physical or mental adjustment or response. Stress can have an external or an internal cause. Any event that you consider a threat and that you find difficult to handle with your current coping strategies or resources could cause you to feel stressed. When someone feels stressed, the "fight or flight" response is triggered. Could it be that some French women's bodies are genetically different from those of the rest of the human race? Does stress not trigger the "fight/flight" response in their bodies? Of course, it does. Could it be that they have found an effective way of coping with this automatic reaction? I think this is much more likely.

The "flight/flight" reaction is an appropriate response to a life-threatening situation. As long as it is followed by physical and mental action to preserve life and a period of rest to reflect and recharge your batteries. We have depended on the "fight/flight" reaction for our survival since pre-historic times. But if the "fight/flight" response is constantly triggered by a perceived threat, whether real or imaginary, without a physical response or a period of rest and recuperation, our physical and mental health can be damaged. Permanently, if the stress is inflicted for long enough.

The problem is that as the "flight/fight" reaction is automatic, people think that they have no control over their reaction to it either. This is not true. Even if the "fight/flight" reaction is triggered automatically, we can choose how we respond to it. We can choose to become distressed. Or we can choose to stay calm. I think this is the secret of some French women's enviable ability to remain unfrazzled while coping with an amount of stress that would drive most other people up the wall.

I have a friend like that. Imperturbable, no matter what happens. She exasperates me.

Most of us are aware, from personal experience, that there are two types of stress – acute stress and chronic stress. Acute stress is what you feel when something suddenly and unexpectedly goes wrong. You feel this sort of stress when your car breaks down on a busy highway during rush hour. Chronic stress is usually present over a longer period of time. It ebbs and flows but never disappears completely. Sometimes it gradually and insidiously increases over time. It is the sort of stress you feel when your boss asks for more and more results in less and less time when you have limited resources available to you.

The causes of acute/chronic stress can be internal or external. Internal, when your interpretation of an event causes stress. External, when the threat is from your environment. Clearly, with such very different origins, there is no one-size-fits-all solution to coping with stress. Even so, there are a few things that I have noticed that French women are less likely to do than the rest of us.

Maybe you are one of those people who constantly reassure yourself that your current high level of stress is temporary. You say to yourself, "I am just extremely busy right now." My friend Amelie would never let this sort of thing happen to her. I once had lunch with her in a restaurant. A perfectly good restaurant, one that we had been to many times before and never had any complaints about. Not that day. That day, Amelie found that her steak had not been cooked to her liking. She did not get stressed about it. She simply sent the steak back six times before she was satisfied with the way that it had been cooked. Did she get irritated? No. Did the waiter get irritated? No. Did the owner of the restaurant get irritated? No. Did the chef get irritated? Probably, but then great chefs are expected to be more volatile than average mortals. Apart from the chef, no one allowed themselves to get stressed. There was no fighting, although I did consider fleeing, more than once.

Or are you someone who blindly accepts stress as permanently part of your life - "I am always busy. I always have lots of things on my plate" - or as part of your identity - "I am highly strung. I just do not cope well with stress"? Amelie would never accept stress as a normal part of her life. She might be highly strung. In fact, she certainly is, but when she starts to feel stressed, she does something about it. In an emergency, she might book herself into a spa for a week and to hell with the consequences. It rarely comes to that, because, being highly strung, she knows that she has to take extra good care of herself. She treats herself to a week at our favourite spa twice a year, in autumn and in spring. This exasperates me too because I am usually the one who had to go with her. It often involves detoxing, and I am convinced that detoxing is of much use. I do usually get a lot writing done during this week, so my time there isn't totally wasted. These days, living I live in the south of France, I have the perfect excuse. Living here is so relaxing that I definitely do not need to escape for a week to a spa.

You might constantly blame your stress on other people and feel that there is nothing you can do about it. You may be convinced that you have no time to do anything about the stress that threatens to overwhelm you.

You may have a problem. Sustained stress can cause or worsen physical illness, sometimes with drastic consequences. Our bodies can only take so much abuse before something gives.

Some people feel that it is not their fault that they are stressed. Sometimes this is true, but more often we are responsible for at least some of the stress we subject ourselves to, even if it is only because of the way we interpret events. In the same situation, one person will be unbearably stressed. Another, like Amelie, with a good range of coping strategies, will barely notice. Unless we take responsibility for our own contribution to the stress that we experience, we will be unable to reduce it.

I don't know if you have ever heard of Marcus Aurelius. If you haven't, it doesn't matter. Please don't stress about it. He was some or other important person who lived nearly 2000 years ago, give or take a couple of centuries. What is interesting, is that he had already figured out at least one very important stress management tactic, all those years ago. He said, "If you are distressed by anything external, the pain is not due to the thing itself, but to your estimate of it; and this you have the power to revoke at any moment."

I asked Amelie how she manages to cope with stress so well. It is quite clear to me that a super-stressed person is going to find it difficult, at the same time, to be a super-confident person. I was expecting her to explain that she had been taught a variety of highly effective stress management strategies. She had, and she eventually discussed these strategies with me. But when I first popped the question, she had only one thing on her mind: getting to know a certain very attractive psychologist better.

"Why on earth do you need a psychologist?", I asked.

"I do not need a psychologist."

"Why are you seeing this chap then?"

"Because this is the only way I could think of to get him to notice me." I should have known.

I had to sigh, "You know, Amelie, this is really most unethical. Well, what happened? Did he notice you?"

"Not really. He is so professional. He has taught me something useful about stress, though. That is why I went to see him. I said I was feeling very stressed lately, and that I needed help to feel less stressed."

The irony. Another sigh from me.

She continued, "He said that the best place to start if I want to learn how to manage my stress better would be to keep a stress diary. This will help me figure out if I am making my stress worse than it actually is. I might be doing this by ignoring my stress, by rationalising it or by blaming it on someone else. A stress diary could help me identify regular stressors in my life. It could reveal the way I currently deal with them. Or not. He said I might already have a couple of effective coping strategies. (If only he knew!) I just need to fine-tune them. Some people, he said, have ineffective coping strategies. Others do not have any coping strategies at all. Can you imagine that? He said some people feel that they do not have time to implement their well-thought-out strategies. Isn't he amazing?"

Amelie's sexy psychologist told her to make a note in her diary each time she felt stressed. I have used the same method to help patients deal with stress. It is very effective. If you have difficulty coping with stress, you may want to give this a go too. When you feel stressed, I suggest you note

- what made you feel stressed,
- how you felt, both physically and emotionally,
- how you reacted and
- what you did to reduce the stress.

Keeping a stress diary takes time, but you do not have to do it for long. Only until a clear pattern emerges of how you manage stress. Your stress diary may reveal that your current stress management strategies are neither effective nor sustainable, even though they make you feel better in the short term. When some people are stressed, they bite their nails. Some smoke, drink too much, binge eat, take drugs, sit in front of their computers or televisions for hours, withdraw from friends and family, take it out on others or go and hide in a dark corner. These are popular "coping strategies" that can cause even worse physical and mental problems than the stress can. If you discover that your stress reducing strategies are not helpful, you can substitute them with more useful strategies.

Amelie's psychologist gave her a few more tips.

- He told her to get daily exercise. She had to choose an activity that she enjoys, that she would be able to keep up in the long run. He suggested going for long walks. It is true that walking is one of the easiest exercises to work into your day. Amelie already walks many miles every week. She loves going for long walks in the countryside anyway, so this was not particularly helpful. She did wonder whether he might enjoy going for long walks in the countryside too...

- He also told her to eat a healthy diet. He said well-nourished bodies are better prepared to cope with stress. She should be mindful of what she eats. She must make sure she gets all the vitamins and minerals she needs. He advised against polluting her body with junk food. As if she ever would! Where possible, he suggested eating organic, in-season, home-grown and home-made food. He encouraged her to drink enough water, throughout the day. I started to warm towards the guy. He was talking a lot of sense.
- He suggested reducing or even cutting out caffeine and sugar altogether. By reducing the amount of coffee and sweet snacks in her diet, Amelie would avoid the mind-boggling sugar and caffeine highs, followed by the crashing blood sugar and caffeine-deprivation lows. Amelie only ever drank a single cup of coffee first thing in the morning. She avoids refined sugar like the plague and severely limits her chocolate consumption.
- No alcohol, no cigarettes and no recreational drugs, he said. Self-medicating with alcohol or drugs may reduce stress temporarily, but it creates additional problems in the long run. Amelie needs a clear mind to deal with the causes of her stress. This did not go down so well. No problem avoiding cigarettes and recreational drugs. But wine? No wine? At all? This did not sound right to Amelie. Of course, one would never overindulge, but to give up the glass of her favourite red that she has with her lunch? She really didn't think she could.
- He advised her to make sure she gets enough sleep. Adequate sleep is essential for a healthy body and mind. Lack of sleep and the resulting tiredness make it more difficult to face stressful challenges. At this, Amelie's imagination ran wild. All that talk about beds and bodies.

> She took in absolutely nothing of whatever else he may have suggested.

I can think of a few more things he may have mentioned.

It is important to build a solid and reliable social support network. French women are generally very good at this. Coping with stress is easier if you have made time for your friends and family. If you are there for them when they need you, they will be there for you when you need them. Talking a stressful situation through with a friend or family member can help you understand exactly what happened. It can help you organise your thoughts. Talking it through can help you process the experience. You may come across surprising insights. Or you may encounter a different interpretation of the problem. There is nothing wrong with asking for help when you need it. You can ask for help from friends and family, but also from professionals like councillors, coaches, psychologists, and doctors.

If you are not sure of how stressed you are, you can complete a simple StressQuiz that you will find on this page at my website: https://wp.me/P829iE-7d.

It is OK to say no and to say no without explaining yourself. If you need to say no to avoid feeling stressed, do so whenever practically possible. If you know a certain situation or person stresses you, avoid that situation/person if you can. Set clear boundaries to protect yourself. If a situation stresses you, try looking at it from a different perspective. Maybe from another person's viewpoint? If you can't change the situation, maybe you can change the way you react. It might help to stand back and take in the bigger picture. Look for compromises.

Try not to

- always expect the worst possible outcome,
- generalise - if you failed at something once, you are convinced you always will,
- focus only on the negatives - you concentrate on what went wrong, you ignore what went right,
- make assumptions or jump to conclusions without proof,
- let your emotions change your interpretation of reality,

- label yourself or others.

As I mentioned in the previous chapter, efficient time management is another great stress-minimising strategy. There are loads of books and articles on and off-line about time management. One of the main reasons we feel stressed is because we feel we do not have enough time to do the things expected of us. Often, we can create extra time for ourselves by managing our time better. By saying no to an invitation that we do not really want to accept. By not wasting time daydreaming or worrying. If you find it impossible not to worry, then limit the time you spend doing it. Choose a specific time, say half an hour a day, from 19h00 to 19h30, to worry. If you start to worry about something during the day, make a note to worry about it later during your "worry time." In the meantime, forget about it. Feeling in control of your worrying is a liberating experience.

Mindfulness can also be a useful ally. Mindfulness can help you break free from stress by fixating your attention on the present moment. You observe and acknowledge your stressful thoughts without reacting to them. You stand back and take note of them but do not engage with them. If you find yourself engaging with a worrying thought, disengage from it. Let it go and bring your attention back to the present moment. You can do this by concentrating on your breathing, for example. Even though practising mindfulness is a simple concept, it is not easy. It takes time to develop this skill.

Each of us is different, each of us has a different way of relaxing. It is useful to make a list of activities that work for you. Put it somewhere obvious, where you can easily access it. Some people like to take a warm, relaxing bath, with candles and soothing music. Others prefer a long walk on the beach or in the countryside. Some enjoy a creative hobby. Others choose to spend time with their friends. Some people pray and read the Bible. Others like to go to a spa and have a massage. We all have something we can do to cope better with stress.

Having said all this, it is useful to remember that a certain amount of stress is essential to our well-being. Most of us perform better under some pressure, often exceeding our expectations of what we are capable of achieving. It is only when we have more stress than we can handle and insufficient time to accommodate change that stress can be damaging to our physical and mental health.

Amelie nearly did get frazzled when her favourite psychologist abruptly terminated their sessions together. He firmly told her that he could help her no further. Amelie is one of those French women who cope with stress by talking things through with her friends. We listened patiently while sipping some of Amelie's favourite red wine. We offered support and encouragement. We did this at whatever time of day or night it was required.

We all went out together to our favourite restaurant (see the steak incident above) for a celebratory lunch when Amelie's psychologist rang her three weeks later and invited her to go for a walk in the country.

I recently published a post on my blog with a list of the ways I deal with stress. Maybe some of these can be of use to you too:

I listen to a guided meditation. Meditating is not easy, especially if you have never done it before. Even if you have never meditated before, a short, guided meditation can help a lot. I consult YouTube. TheHonestGuys do an excellent, short (10 min) Mindful Meditation that does the trick for me. You can choose a guided meditation from the list on my Margaretha Montagu YouTube channel.

Spending time with a pet can be relaxing. Cats, dogs, horses – all have been used as animal therapists. You can sit quietly and stroke your cat, or you can take the dog out for a run. I saddle up and go for a ride. The countryside here is so beautiful, it always soothes me. The idea is to take your mind off whatever is stressing you.

You could lose yourself in a book or a film. This doesn't always work for me. Sometimes I am just too stressed to concentrate.

I often fall back on this excellent sense of humour that I have been carefully nurturing all these years. I try to see the funny side (assuming there is one,) I watch a comedy. I read a funny book. I remind myself of something funny that happened to me. I watch a comedy/stand-up comic. I do a Google search for jokes about doctors. I phone a friend who makes me laugh. Sometimes I read one of the blogs that I following because the author has such a contagious sense of humour.

It can occasionally work to talk it over with someone I trust. I choose an emphatic but encouraging sort of person. Otherwise, I end up more stressed afterwards than I was before. Talking it through with someone who is objective can be useful. Other people can often offer you a different and maybe less stressful perspective.

Listening to music can make me feel less stressed. On YouTube, there are loads of different types of music to choose from. There are even guided music meditations.

When it all becomes too much, I pray. The first thing I always do (or just about always, from time to time I forget), is to pray. Within months of arriving, our rescue horse Leo got colic. As any horse owner will tell you, this is very bad news. Not many horses survive a colic attack. Leo was fine until 1pm. By 2pm he was rolling on the ground in agony, groaning with pain. My stress levels went from low to sky-high. We desperately tried to convince Leo to get up and walk, as the vet suggested. But getting anywhere near to scared-to-death-of-abusive-humans Leo was close to impossible. He got steadily weaker and finally the vet managed to give him an intravenous injection to try and ease the obstruction in his gut.

Over the next 48 hours, I spend most of my time with him - day and night. He eventually gave up trying to get away from me and ended up on his side with his head in my lap. I spent hours talking to him quietly, stroking whichever part of him I could reach. For the first time ever, I got to touch his lower legs, where the scars from being shackled are still visible. It was heart-breaking. After months of trying to win his trust, he would now become distressed if I as much as get up to go to the loo, whinnying weakly for me not to leave him.

I spent many of those hours praying...and against all expectations, two days later, he seemed to rally round. He ate a bit of hay and drank a bit of water. He got up slowly, leaning heavily on me and took a few faltering steps. It took a long time, but he did get better.

You can also choose to write stress out of your system. A bit like I did above. Any piece of paper will do, even a paper napkin or a beer coaster. I speak from personal experience here. I like to get things out of my head and onto paper. When I am so stressed that I can't write about it, I make a list of the things that I am grateful for. When I am super-stressed, this is not easy. Even so, there is always something to be grateful for. Regularly listing the things that you are thankful for can be an effective long-term stress management tool.

Doing something creative can take my mind off my worries. Some people paint, others make pots. I can't paint or draw pictures, but I love giving old pieces of furniture a new lease of life with a coat of chalk paint. Our house is half-timbered. With all these dark oak beams, the last thing we need is another piece of dark wood furniture. A lot of my flea market finds end up with a coat of white paint. Needless to say, I love lowering my stress levels by browsing second-hand shops and flea markets.

I am convinced that knowing how to manage stress can help anyone feel more confident. This is what the Connect with Horses Personal Empowerment workshops that we host with the help of our horses here in the south of France are all about. Equine-assisted experiential learning enables our guests to develop new coping strategies by working with the horses. No one does any riding. We do the exercises with everyone's feet firmly on the ground. The exercises are designed to enable participants to build their confidence in a very practical way.

For the stress management sessions, we often enlist the help of our Tinker stallion Bass des Sources Sacrées. Bass is a very big horse with a huge personality. Most of our guest feel anxious when asked to do an exercise with Bass, but Bass is a gentle giant. He is infinitely patient. He gives his human partner the time to overcome her fear of him. Initially, he resists all her attempts to get him to participate. The moment she overcomes her fear, he gives her his full cooperation. His technique is extremely successful. His human partner invariably feels ten feet taller once she manages to get him to work with her.

We also introduce our guests to various meditation methods, including equine-guided meditation, to help them find a method that suits them and that will enable them to continue to handle stress effectively when they get home. Many of our guests have said that the workshop had been a life-changing experience.

In the next chapter, my friend Inès tackles a very difficult subject: How to forgive the unforgivable.

Chapter 7

Forgiveness

Inès remembers the first time her father sexually abused her well. It was on her sixth birthday. Inès and her mother had been to the shops a couple of days before her birthday. Inès had chosen the perfect dress for her birthday party, a pink princess dress with a tight bodice and a flowing skirt. She can remember to this day the silky feel of that skirt and the way it swirled around her legs as she twirled in front of the mirror. On the morning of her birthday, her mother brought her breakfast in bed, and she opened up all her presents. Her father had to be at work early, so he could not join in the fun. She remembers regretting that he could not be there that morning.

Later that afternoon, several of Inès's friends came to her birthday party. They all arrived looking like fairy princesses in their best party dresses. Inès's dress was the most beautiful. The party was a huge success. Inès had asked for a cupcake tower as a birthday cake. She can still remember the glorious taste of those giant cupcakes. Even the sweet strawberry smell still lingers in her memory. Inès's father had taken the afternoon off to attend his little girl's birthday party. Inès's happiness was complete when he arrived halfway through the party. He grabbed her and threw her high up in the air in front of all her friends. It was clear to everyone that he loved his little princess very much.

That is probably why what happened later that night hurt so much, in so very many different ways. The abuse went on for the next five years. Sometimes every night, sometimes once a week, but rarely less frequently than that.

Inès and I met when we were in post-graduate medical school together. I admired Inès. She had style. She always dresses beautifully in a seemingly effortless way. She has an irresistible accent and what she has to say always made a lot of sense. She looks so together, so in control of herself and of her surroundings. So elegant. So mature. So confident. It was clear that she came from a privileged background where money was no object. Bon chic, bon genre, if you see what I mean.

Inès was an only child. When we met, she still lived with her parents in the family chateau. She came to stay with me frequently, but we rarely went to stay at her parents' house. I was married by then and preferred to stay close to my home, so it never bothered me. When I did visit her, it was always for some or other occasion. It was for her mother's birthday party, a charity ball or a fund-raising dinner. Busy weekends, I seem to remember. She never mentioned the abuse. It was only when I asked her about confidence, many years later, that I got an inkling of what had happened all those years ago.

I never suspected. Inès is one of the most confident, accomplished and self-possessed women I know. It was clear to everyone, right from the start, that Inès would go far. Admittedly, she was a very private person, with only a handful of close friends. I put this down to her aversion of seeing her own name in the newspapers. Her family's wealth and standing meant that she was frequently a target of the "gutter press," as she described them.

"Confidence?" she said, "You want to talk about confidence? I suppose you think that I am confident because I had a privileged upbringing and because I always had the very best that money could buy? Not so, dear friend. If I am confident, it is despite my so-called privileged upbringing. My father abused me sexually, during my childhood. If I am confident today, it is because I finally managed to forgive him. I forgave him instead of allowing the festering hatred that I felt for him to poison my every waking moment."

I looked at her for a long time while slowly each piece of the puzzle that was Inès fell into place. She waited patiently until she saw the last piece had found its home. "I could have allowed what he did to destroy me. For a long time, it eradicated every shred of self-confidence I might have developed. But what good is always living in the past? I was lucky. I got help." She laughs hollowly. "In today's anti-religious climate, you may be surprised to hear that it was my confessor who saved me from a life of bitterness. In my late teens, at my wits' end, I drummed up the courage to talk to him. Against all my expectations, he not only believed me, he immediately arranged for me to be counselled. He found a fully-qualified pastoral counsellor with a lot of experience of working in this field. She saved my life. With her help, I came to understand that hating someone as much as I hated my father and yearning for revenge with every fibre of my being is indeed like drinking poison and hoping he would die. Of course, it does not happen. It only poisoned my own existence. I am not saying that it was easy. It took a long time. Many sessions. A lot of back-tracking. A lot of tears. Getting to the point where I was ready to forgive was hard work. Very hard work.

In the end, I did. It was liberating. I remember exactly where I was and what I was doing when I finally decided to forgive my father. And my mother. When I feel myself slipping back, I imagine myself back there. I relive that liberating feeling in its full intensity. The past is behind me. The present is here to enjoyed and the future is there to look forward to. I will never allow anyone to steal this from me again. I am confident now that I am worthy of love and respect. Maybe confidence that has been lost and had to be rebuilt, from scratch, is the strongest type of confidence of there is."

I suspect that Inès may be right about this. Are all French women able to forgive? I doubt it. I do know one who has managed it and who taught me the importance of not letting your past eat away at your self-esteem.

Recently, much has been written about the "mother wound." As far as I can understand, a "mother wound" refers to the emotional trauma caused in a child's mind by a significant dysfunction in the relationship with the child's mother. This is often caused by the mother having suffered similar trauma in her childhood. This sort of thing, I am sure, can affect both boys and girls, but most is written about the effect it has on adult women. I am also sure that similar emotional trauma can be caused by a "father wound," affecting both adult men and women, but most of the research I have done on this subject focused on the effect it has on mature women.

I learnt in medical school that inadequate nurturing – by one or by both parents - can affect children's ability to form nurturing relationships. This is perfectly understandable and there is nothing new in that. The child of an emotionally distant, inconsistent or hypercritical mother does not feel loved. The child ends up feeling unworthy of affection and attention. This results in an insecure and ambivalent attachment of the child to the parent. We know that early childhood attachments are highly predictive of all adult relationships. Especially of romantic relationships.

This lack of secure attachment in childhood often causes a formidable lack of self-confidence in adulthood. It is not surprising that such a child becomes convinced that he/she is neither lovable nor worthy of attention. This undermines his/her self-confidence, causing the child to deny its own talents and abilities. Even gifted children often fail to accomplish anything at all.

Are you still yearning for your mother's love, love that you did not receive as a child? I think it is important to take on board that you may never heal this relationship. What you can do, is heal from the damage that this inadequate relationship has caused. It is unlikely that your mother is going to change without intensive therapy. You need to let go of that yearning for a nurturing relationship with your mother. You can heal your "mother wound" or "father wound" by learning to mother/father your inner child. You will feel dramatically more confident once you manage to do this. I would suggest putting yourself in the hands of a professional with many years of experience. Just like Inès did.

We are not damaged because we did not receive love in the past. We are damaged because we do not love ourselves in the present.

Chances are good that you have been hurt by another person at least once in your life. Mostly, we get over the sort of thing fairly quickly, and we manage to move on. But not always. Sometimes we cannot let go, and the hurt continues to fester. Pain caused us in the past can poison our present, and it can poison our future. It can be so distracting that we lose our jobs. It can destroy our relationships with our friends and our family. It can severely undermine our self-confidence.

If you can forgive, you can get your life back on track. Forgiving someone does not mean you forget what has happened. Forgiveness does not sanction what the other person did. It does not mean the other person will apologise. It does not mean that the other person will change. All it means is that you are letting go of the pain this person's acts have caused.

I have mentioned our little rescue horse, Aurileo d'Alegria, in the last chapter. We rescued Leo from the front court of the abattoir. Leo is a very beautiful dappled palomino. He used to be a bull-fighter. He has a huge scar halfway down his neck where I suspect a bull's horn went in. There is a similar wound on the other side of his neck. He also has nasty, festering scars around all four his lower legs, where we think they shackled him at the abattoir to keep him from running away. He has scars on his sides, probably from too-sharp spurs and old whip-mark scars across his rump. He also has scars on his face.

When he first arrived, people scared Leo out of his mind. It was impossible to get anywhere near him. He would occasionally allow himself to be caught when bribed with carrots, but he would never voluntarily approach a human. We decided to give him time and to wait until he was ready to come to us. It took nearly a year.

One night, nearly a year after Leo's arrival and long after darkness fell, our farrier came to see one of our mares. Belle had developed a hoof abscess and was in a lot of pain. The farrier came after a hard day's work to drain the abscess. During the day, she had made it very clear that she was suffering horribly and Leo stuck to her side like super-glue.

Due to the late hour, only the area immediately around Belle was lit. The farrier decided that he would do the job in the field where the horses were. The rest of the herd was milling about in sympathy, especially Belle's daughter Aurore. The procedure was complicated and took a while. At some point, I leaned back against Aurore. I often do this. Aurore has been with us since birth, and she is quite willing to be leaned against for extended periods. I leaned against her for several minutes, enjoying the warmth. At some point, I turned towards her to put my arm over her back...only to find she had suddenly shrunk at least 20 cm.

Great was my surprise when I saw that it was Leo, I had been leaning against all along! If I am telling you this story, it is because, to this day, I remain in awe of this little horse's capacity to forgive. Having been overworked, beaten, shackled and starved to near-death, he still found the courage somewhere in his huge heart to forgive people for what they had done to him. He reached out towards us, tentatively, furtively and then more and more confidently as it became clear to him that we meant him no harm. It took him nearly a year, but he managed to put the past behind him, to forgive and maybe even to forget.

Forgiving is not easy. It may feel impossible. But it can be done, if not on your own, then with the help of a professional and experienced therapist. If you want to give it a go on your own, there are a few things that you can do:

1. Make up your mind and let it go. Do this for your own sake. The anger you fell prevents you from healing. It imprisons you in the past. You cannot control other people's actions, but you can choose how you are going to react. You can choose to let it go and start the healing process.
2. Think about the effect that all this anger, resentment and pain have on you. Being angry uses up a lot of energy. When you are angry, your body is at the mercy of hormones that prepare you for the impending fight or flight. In other words, you are stressed, not only mentally but also physically. This can harm your health. It can harm your relationships with others.
3. It might help to think about the things that you yourself may need forgiveness for. If we can admit that we may have done things in the past that we need forgiveness for, it makes it easier to contemplate forgiving someone in the present.
4. Sometimes, it helps to look at what happened from the other person's viewpoint, to put yourself in the other person's shoes. What could have happened to him/her in the past that caused him/her to hurt you? Could you be partly responsible for what has happened? This does not mean that you are shouldering part of the blame. It just stops you from feeling like a helpless victim. None of this, of course, can be applied to abuse of any kind. Knowing why something happened can be useful, but it is not essential to know why a person behaved badly to be able to forgive this person.
5. Do not suppress your emotions. Acknowledge your anger, your frustration, your depression, your feeling of helplessness. It can help a lot to write your feelings down. It may help to write a letter to the person who hurt you, a letter

that you never intend to send. You can then destroy this letter, symbolically destroying the pain this person has caused you.
6. Should your emotions become overwhelming, use one of the stress management techniques we discussed in the previous chapter to re-balance yourself.
7. Focus on the things you have to be grateful for. It is so easy to forget your blessings when you are hurt and angry. Make a concerted effort to focus on the things that make you happy.

It might be one of the most challenging things you will ever do, but it can be done. I do not know if French women are any better at forgiving than the rest of us. What I do know is holding a grudge, however valid, dramatically diminishes your self-confidence, slowly but surely. The decision is yours and yours only. When you forgive someone, you are doing it for your own physical and mental (and spiritual) well-being and for your own peace of mind. If you have tried but cannot resolve this issue on your own, please get professional help.

In the next chapter, you will meet my friend Monique. Monique explains how she has managed to stay self-assured and assertive as she got older.

Chapter 8

Confronting Age

As we get older, we may start to feel less confident. We may start to doubt our attractiveness and our abilities. Our bodies change as we get older, there is no denying it. Is there no other option but to feel less confident as we get older? There definitely is. I have noticed that many French women's confidence does not waver as they grow older. On the contrary, they seem to become even more confident as they mature.

I have long suspected that French women's confidence have a lot to do with their seemingly effortless ability to find joy in the present moment. Could this be the secret of their much-envied "joie de vivre," especially as they get older? Mindfulness can be a great confidence-builder and stress-buster. Problems have arisen in modern day-to-day life because we have allowed ourselves to disconnect from the here-and-now. We have become focused solely on mindless activity. We dwell either in the future or in the past. Although as we get older, we may reflect more and rush around less.

I definitely have become more contemplative as I got older. With the big fifty looming large on the horizon, I started to ponder the French approach to ageing. Age does not seem to have the same meaning to French women as it has for women of some other cultures. Some French women seem to have discovered the secret of ageing confidently.

Ageing here seems to have fewer negative implications than elsewhere, especially for women. I have a friend who ran a successful boutique hotel for 35 years in one of the Mediterranean coast's most fashionable resorts. She and her husband have recently sold their hotel and have moved to Gascony (our region). They now run a much smaller but just as smart chateau as a four-star bed-and-breakfast.

Monique always takes my breath away when I see her. Over sixty, she still wears her thick hair loose and long, all the way down her back. No longer blond, she has settled for a silver sheen, with the vaguest suggestion of the gold-blond of her youth. She admitted to me in an unguarded moment that it costs her a small fortune to keep it like that. She wears full battle camouflage from the moment she gets up until seconds before she goes to sleep. She still favours the full palette, à la Brigitte Bardot. The only concession she has made is that she no longer wears false eyelashes. She cannot be described as thin. Trim would be more appropriate. She dresses extravagantly but elegantly. Quite a combination to pull off, let me assure you. Which she does, with tremendous flair.

Monique, way over sixty, still stops the traffic. She stops the conversation when she walks into a room. Men jump up to pull out a chair for her or to open a door for her. Waiters and taxis appear as if by magic at her elbow. They get that slightly dazed look that men often get in the presence of a beautiful woman. That is just the thing, you see. Monique still is, and plans to be for many years yet, a beautiful woman who commands attention from wherever she goes. She could easily have looked grotesque, but she does not. Not even remotely. I have spent a fair amount of time trying to work out how she does it.

I have finally come to the conclusion that her secret is never to take herself too seriously, nor anyone else for that matter. Monique has got a sense of humour that makes her one of the easiest and most enjoyable people to be with. Her one-liners are legendary. She makes people laugh. Should you walk past a sidewalk café and hear a burst of unrestrained laughter coming from inside, stop and go in. You are sure to find Monique there, holding court. When Monique leaves a room, it feels as if the heating has just been switched off.

One afternoon, as we were sitting under the two-hundred-year-old oak tree in our front courtyard, looking out over the horses' paddocks, I pinned her down. I asked her directly what the secret of her age-undiminished confidence was.

"Eh bien;" she said, "I think it is all about attention to detail."

I stared dumbfounded. Detail? What detail?

She smiled indulgently. "Remaining confident as you get older is all about paying attention to detail. Not letting anything go south. Not anything, do you understand? Of course, you tone things down a bit. (What a sensation she must have been when she was young if this is the toned-down version!) I no longer wear my nails long and painted with scarlet nail polish. Of course not. But I take care of my hands and nails with even more dedication than I did when I was younger. Same goes for my skin. My hair. My clothes. I pay attention to the small details. What do you call it these days? The new buzzword? Mindfulness. I am mindful of the details.

I think the whole mindfulness movement has arrived just in time. Being mindful has always come naturally to me and not just where my appearance is concerned. I am as mindful of other people as I am of myself. I listen to what people say to me. I pay attention to their posture, their changing expressions, their reactions to their surroundings. I pay attention to my surroundings, in detail. I pay attention to atmosphere. To ambiance, or to the lack of it.

The past is long gone, tu sais, and I don't have any regrets. The future is not here yet, so why dwell on it? 'Now' is where everything is happening. 'Now' is where happiness lives, only waiting to be unveiled. Yes, this mindfulness-malarkey suits me well. I think it would suit most French women. When I pay attention to the details, I feel confident. I feel confident that I look good. I feel confident that my house looks good. I feel confident that the b-and-b looks good.

If I remain attractive, I think it is because I am a good listener. I think attentive listening is key to all effective communication. When people do not listen properly, they misunderstand each other. Communication breaks down. Listening, with all your heart, requires focus and concentration. The problem these days is, I am convinced, that most people do not listen with the intent to understand, they listen with the intent to reply.

When you are a good listener, you pay attention to the details. You are mindful not only of what is being said but also of how it is being said. Of what is not being said. Of both verbal and non-verbal communication. When you listen in this way to people, they feel important. One of the biggest compliments you can give another person is to listen to what they are saying with total absorption.

They reward you with devotion. How could anyone not be confident with all this devotion being aimed at them? Maybe the secret of French women's enduring confidence as they get older is their ability to listen intently. I am sure that is what bound the infamous French kings to their equally famous and influential mistresses.

Enough about me. I understand that you are seriously into mindfulness too? Tell me more about this mindfulness and these mindful self-empowerment workshops that you host. We can compare ideas and see if my old-fashioned 'paying attention to detail' is the same as your mindfulness."

Monique's other secret is that she is extremely good at making other people talk about themselves! While she listened attentively, I tried to put my ideas into words: "Let me explain it the way I usually explain it to our workshop participants. Mindfulness is all about focusing on the present moment. It is about noticing the sights, smells, sounds and tastes that one experiences, as well as the thoughts and feelings one has from one moment to the next. It can help us appreciate our environment and each other. It can help us understand ourselves better.

To be mindful means to be unconditionally present. As far as I can gather, mindfulness is about paying precise and non-judgemental attention to the details of our experiences. Which I think, is exactly what you said, didn't you? Instead of struggling to get away from experiences we find difficult to cope with, we remain present in the moment."

I have read quite a bit about mindfulness. I have read what Prof Jon Kabat-Zinn has to say in his book "Where ever you go, there you are." I have read what Prof Mark Williams has to say in his book "Mindfulness: A practical guide to finding peace in a frantic world." Prof Williams says that it is easy to stop noticing the world around us. He says that it is easy to lose touch with the way our bodies are feeling and to end up living in our heads. We become so busy with our thoughts that we lose sight of how those thoughts are driving our emotions and our reactions. That would fit in with what you said about listening, wouldn't it? When we live in our heads, we cannot possibly listen properly.

Monique poured another cup of tea and thought for a while. "Yes," she says, "I can see where this meets my own convictions. But how can your 'mindfulness' help your workshop participants feel more confident and manage stress better? If I understand you correctly, this is what your workshops are about? Confidence and stress management? Because the ability to manage stress makes people more confident? I have certainly found that when I have all the details in sight, I feel much less stressed. And much more confident. Is that how it works?"

"Not exactly. The mindfulness I tell people about during our workshops is about being mindful of themselves, their thoughts, their feelings. When we are not mindful of our thoughts and feelings, we sometimes react in disastrous ways. When we are mindful of ourselves, we are aware of our thoughts and emotions. Mindfulness can help us identify thought patterns that lead to indiscriminate reactions.

In this way, mindfulness can help us to become more aware of the way we respond to stress. We may notice that we often overreact to a perceived threat. Or even that we perceive a threat where no threat exists. We may realise that we sometimes interpret a neutral situation as a threatening one. We might have to acknowledge that we allow our fears (sometimes completely groundless) to dictate our actions.

Once we become aware of these destructive thought patterns and habits, we can do something about them. Mindfulness helps us to discover that we can choose how we are going to react in any given situation. By being mindful, we can train ourselves to change the way we respond, especially in challenging situations. We can then react in a way that is stress-reducing and conducive to our well-being and our health. Does this make sense to you?"

Monique nodded enthusiastically. "Indeed. It makes a lot of sense to me. I can see how I have been unconsciously using this technique to remain confident as I grow older. I think it is normal to start doubting yourself, your abilities and your attractiveness, as you get older. When I start thinking like that, I immediately stop myself. I quickly remind myself of a recent compliment or achievement. I remind myself of everything that I still am and have/ It makes me feel grateful and confident. I think that mindfulness is also about noticing when you start putting yourself down, isn't it?"

I agree with Monique. I think that this may well be the reason why French women remain as confident as ever as they grow older. They might well be less likely to put themselves down and criticise themselves than other women are. They may also be good at managing stress, as we saw in chapter 6. I think that effective stress management is one of the main reasons why the people in this part of France are famous for their healthy longevity.

If you put yourself down constantly, often without registering it, you can use mindfulness to stop doing so. You can re-build your confidence, whatever your age.

In my opinion, being confident means, you accept yourself just as you are, at this very moment. You have faith in your abilities, your competence and in your judgement. We all question ourselves from time to time, especially in challenging situations. When questioning ourselves gives us the opportunity to pause and plan, it has a positive result. When questioning ourselves make us suspect that we are going to fail, it affects us negatively. Mindfulness can make you aware of negative thoughts. It offers you the chance to change the direction that your thoughts are taking. It helps you accept negative thoughts without judgement, and it helps you control how you react to these thoughts. Mindfulness is a powerful path towards a calmer, clearer and more confident mind.

Monique may be careful not to be too self-critical, but she is not blind to her own weaknesses. Monique taught me about self-compassion, about forgiving myself for my own imperfections. It seems to me that self-criticism has become an acceptable way of behaving because it makes us socially acceptable. We criticise ourselves to conform to our (often-imaginary) judges' low opinion of us. Monique suggested doing the exact opposite. She recommends complimenting oneself at least once a day. Preferably much more often than that.

Self-compassion is not just about acknowledging our physical limitations, especially as we get older. It is not just about taking the best possible care of ourselves, physically and mentally. It also involves responding to our insecurity, our frustration and our confusion with kindness and understanding.

One thing I have noticed is that as I get older, I care less and less about what other people think of me. Complimenting myself is easier than it used to be. This year, I will come across that great milestone, my fiftieth birthday. Bonjour, Midlife! Not altogether comfortable with the idea, I had a look on the internet to see how other women are coping with this major life change. What a revelation! I first searched for other midlife bloggers and found a huge community of inspiring women (English and French) and their blogs: Brazen Women, Reclaiming Mary, Still Blonde After All, Midlife Chic, Letters from Midlife, A Boomer's Life After 50, Making Midlife Matter, Empty House Full Mind, Diary Of A Mid-Life Crisis, Hell Bent On Happy and Midlife Maze. I discovered MidlifeBoulevard.com: one of the best places to find other midlife women bloggers.

I also found Facebook pages written by midlife women: Fifty Not Frumpy, Midlife Warrior Sisterhood, Best Knickers Always and Women After 50. I found a couple of Facebook groups that looked interesting: Midlife Bloggers Association, The Women of Midlife and Sassy Midlife Women. I joined and started building a midlife support network. As you do.

My fiftieth birthday no longer looked as intimidating a milestone as it did before. It seems that mid-life is the time to:

- Stop complaining
- Stop criticising yourself and others
- Stop listening to gossip
- Stop making excuses
- Stop procrastinating
- Stop blaming others when things go wrong
- Stop neglecting your own needs
- Stop labelling yourself and other people
- Stop making unverified assumptions
- Stop trying to control everyone and everything around you
- Stop resisting change
- Stop your fear from limiting you

- Stop dwelling on the past
- Stop trying to live up to other people's expectations
- Stop trying to please everyone all the time

I wrote a few blog posts about midlife and how to cope with its challenges. According to researchers, midlife is now defined as the period between ages 35 to 60, so if you fall in this group, you may find blog posts like this one useful: 12 Life-saving Midlife Tips. We also host private personal empowerment workshops exclusively for midlife women. I absolutely adore hosting these, and so does my soul-mare Belle de la Babinière, who at the grand old age of 16 has definitely arrived at midlife too. Belle understands the trials and tribulations of midlife women, being an empty-nester herself (her daughter Aurore is 6 years old now and currently away at dressage college). She lost the love of her life, Beau de la Babinière, a proud Lusitano stallion, to colic in 2014. She is now in a new and very different relationship with the Duc d'Alegria. Her body is changing. She has aches and pains she never had before and she has a lot of trouble with her weight. She fully understands the changes and challenges that midlife brings. No wonder she bonds so firmly with our midlife retreat guests.

The next chapter is about YOU.

Chapter 9

Implementing the French Approach

If you ever want to see the confident French woman in action, I suggest you spend a morning in a French hairdressing salon. Choose a hairdressing salon in a small country town, not one in a city. When you walk through the door, you might venture a hearty "Bonjour Messieurs-Dames!" Do include the "Messieurs." You will be surprised to see how many sturdy agricultural types, of all ages, are comfortably installed in chairs that barely look capable of carrying their weight. You may also be startled to see that these chaps are in no way intimidated by being in this feminine stronghold. On the contrary, they seem to be enjoying themselves tremendously. They actively contribute to the conversation while having their hair cut into the latest style favoured by men of the world. It may seem as if everyone is talking at the same time.

After an enthusiastic "Bonjour, Madame!", you will soon be seated on a canapé while waiting your turn at the mirror. Because you will wait, even if you arrive on time. Everyone going to a hairdresser in France knows that there will be a wait. In fact, they expect to wait and would be seriously put out if they were not allowed to "patienter." The waiting period is very important. It gives you the opportunity to orient yourself in the conversation. You have time to get to grips with the general direction that the conversation is taking. The subject of the conversation will, without a doubt, be about something of importance to women. Everyone will have an opinion, and everyone will have a chance to voice it. Even the men in the room. The fact that everyone may be voicing their opinion at the same time is neither here nor there. That is what the waiting period is there for. It gives you a chance of figuring out what is going on before you join the fray.

Have you ever noticed that French people seem to need to move their hands a lot while talking? I have been told that the way to get a French woman to stop talking is to tie her hands behind her back. Personally, I cannot imagine getting my message across without using my hands. In a hairdressing salon, this habit becomes an elevated art form. When your time comes at the mirror, keep your eyes on the hands of the hairdresser while she cuts your hair. Nowhere else are a pair of scissors used to emphasise a point with such effect, while at the same time managing not to cut your ears off. Not only is there no bloodshed, but your hair gets cut, according to the skill of the stylist, more or less the way you wanted it cut.

Do not forget to have a good look around. Here, in this modest room with the pot plants in the window, you will see several of the characteristics of confident French women in action. Next to you may be sitting a lady of a certain age having her hair cut and coloured. Over her dead body will she be going grey before she dies. There may be a heated conversation going on about the shade she wants. The stylist, a mere girl at 31, will be trying to convince her client that the dark shade favoured by the client will look too harsh at her age. The client, fully aware of the wisdom of this suggestion, would nevertheless not give in without a good fight. Same would go for the colour of the nail polish the manicurist is applying to the client's well-cared for hands. When you reach eighty, you do not immediately succumb to the suggestions made to you by a mere slip of a girl, be she thirty, forty or fifty. You would, after all, have been taking care of yourself for more than seventy years. By now you have a pretty good idea of how to go about it. Information that you would be glad to share, in a loud voice, with all the other customers.

Here you will see the average French woman's typical support system deployed to its full capacity. Three generation may be attending the salon at the same time. The grandmother, the mother and the daughter, all there to support each other. Not as much with the hairdressing as with winning whatever argument brakes out amongst the patrons. Sometimes, there is no argument. Sometimes there is a problem to be solved. If someone has a problem, it will be discussed in detail. A solution will be found, no matter what the problem is. Most people there would have a vast network of friends, family, and contacts. An animated discussion of available options will result in the best possible solution. Help will be offered, generously, without expecting anything in return. Although, you may have to offer help of your own at some future date.

Since everyone knows everyone else and has done so for several generations, withholding any information is useless. With your mother and your grandmother in attendance and probably your father too, it is no use trying to be someone you are not.

You will discover how important self-care is to French women and to French men too. You will discover how little meaning time has in this context. You may still be waiting for your turn three cups of coffee later. You will notice how little stress these people seem to suffer from. You will see how well-respected older women are. You will hear how often their opinion is requested and find out how much weight this opinion carries. You will learn how laughter can diffuse any heated discussion. You will share other people's lives, their highs, their lows, their hopes and their disappointments. You will walk out the door with a new hairdo, feeling cheerful and confident. You would have had the opportunity to say what you think. You would have listened and would have been listened to. You would feel you have made a valuable contribution to your community and that your community appreciate your contribution. All that for the price of a new haircut.

You now have a good idea of how French women manage to remain so serenely confident. You may be thinking that you would like to implement a few of their confidence-boosting tactics and so increase your own self-esteem. You may consider defining exactly who you are. You may decide to take better care of yourself. You may want to bring more balance into your life. You may think of building a stronger support system for yourself. You may desperately want to find out how to manage stress better. Developing a new habit is never easy, especially when there are already a few obstructive habits in place. You will need patience and perseverance. The resulting increase in self-confidence undoubtedly makes it worthwhile, but where does one start? I suggest you decide what you want to work on first. One of the most noticeable ways I have seen women destroy their self-confidence is by constantly criticising themselves. They always seem to feel the need to apologise for some or other (often imaginary) short-coming. Let's assume that you want to get rid of this destructive habit. You want to stop criticising yourself the whole day long. This would be a good place to start.

You may have noticed that you sometimes talk to yourself in a negative way. Many people do. En plus, we are constantly confronted with other people's negative opinions of us.

When we take these opinions on board, we may end up repeating these negative convictions over and over to ourselves. Especially when we were not feeling well, when we are stressed or when we face a challenge. We may even worsen the problem by contributing some negative thoughts of our own.

You may say to yourself: "I am stupid," "I am a loser," "I can never do anything right" or "No one likes me." This is your inner critic talking. You obstinately believe this, no matter how untrue or unreal. Even in the face of evidence to the contrary. When you make a mistake, you immediately think "I am so stupid. How could I have made such an obvious mistake? This proves, yet again, that I am a total idiot." You feel like a fraud. You may fear that if you take pride in your intelligence and abilities you will be rejected by others. You may feel that you constantly have to make sure that whatever you are saying and doing does not offend anyone else. You may feel that you do not deserve to be loved. So many of my workshop participants feel this way that it inspired me to write a book called You ARE Good enough! This book will provide you with a ten-simple-step method that will help you internalise how unique, powerful, gifted, beautiful, strong, generous, appreciated, valuable, talented, brilliant, admired, respected, courageous, special, caring and lovable you are

If you would like to find out how critical you are of yourself, the self-criticism quiz on this page: https://wp.me/P829iE-7d, will tell you. This is your last quiz! Like the others, this quiz is designed to serve as a road map, to give you an idea which areas you need to work on. I am quite keen on the odd quiz. I regularly add a quiz or two to a book or a blog post. If you find them useful too, you can subscribe to my mailing list to receive notice of new blog posts at my website.

You may think these thoughts so often that you are hardly aware of them. If you have difficulty identifying this thought pattern, carry a small notebook with you for a few days. Jot down any negative thoughts about yourself whenever you notice them. Once you become mindful of your negative thoughts, you may want to take a closer look at these thoughts. Decide whether they are valid or not. Ask yourself the following questions about each negative thought that you notice: Is this impression that I have consisted with reality? What benefit do I get by thinking in this way?

Once you have identified your negative thoughts, you can change them. You can choose a set of positive affirmations to repeat to yourself whenever you notice yourself thinking negatively.

The easiest way to start the process would be to set yourself a SMART goal.

Setting and achieving smart goals will boost your self-confidence substantially. Each time you achieve a purposefully set objective, your confidence in your own ability grows. By setting clearly defined goals, you can measure and take pride your achievements.

Confidence results from the experience of achieving our goals. We must have ways to evaluate the goal-setting experience. We need to know whether we were successful or not. This is where SMART and SMARTER goals come in.

SMART goals are:

Specific: The idea is to state your goal as a positive and unambiguous statement: "I am going to stop putting myself down."

Measurable: The goal should be broken down into smaller, clear-cut steps. "I am going to pay attention to my inner critic for an hour every day for a week," then for two hours a day, then for three hours a day etc.

Attainable: Make sure the goal fits in with your work, friends, family and personal commitments. "I will do this exercise at a time when it will not interfere with my other commitments" - until it becomes a habit that I am no longer conscious of.

Relevant and Realistic: A goal should be physically and mentally possible. There is nothing more dispiriting than failing to achieve an unrealistic goal. Make sure you have enough time, money, resources and support to achieve your goal. It is perfectly possible to pay attention to your inner critic for an hour every day and to call a halt the moment you realise that your inner critic is reprimanding you. You can then replace your negative thoughts with a positive affirmation: "I am confident in all that I do. I do my best in everything I undertake."

Time-bound: Decide when you will have achieved each small step on the way to your final goal. Choose the date that you aim to finalise each step. Make a note on a calendar. "I will increase my awareness of my inner critic with an hour every week for the next 8 weeks." If your goals are not time-bound, you could become paralysed by procrastination. You could end up more frustrated and unfocused than before you started.

Exciting and motivating: "Not putting myself down constantly will make me confident enough to ask for the raise that I know I deserve."

Recorded and Reviewed: Setting goals work better when you write them down, if only for the pleasure of drawing a line through the goal when you achieve it. It is also a good idea to review your goals frequently to make sure that they remain SMART and to check your progress often.

Effective goal-setting can build self-confidence by:

- providing you with a way to measure your progress,
- clarifying your expectations,
- focusing your attention,
- enabling you reach small targets on the way to your final goal,
- thus, increasing your motivation to achieve your goal.

Setting a goal to stop criticising yourself is a worthwhile exercise if you would like to become more confident and assertive. The next step would be to replace your negative thoughts with a few carefully constructed positive statements of intent. These statements or affirmations can enable you to imprint your mind with a new way of thinking. Keep in mind that this sort of re-programming takes time. Do not expect substantial improvement in exchange for minimum input. Repeat your affirmations daily. For the best results, you will have to do so for at least 6 weeks.

You do not have to believe your affirmations. All you have to do is to repeat them. However, if they are too unrealistic, your mind will reject them. Take the statement "I am supremely confident." If you are nothing of the sort, you are going to find this difficult to take on board. The statement "I choose to be supremely confident" is much more believable and thus much more powerful.

Try to think like a French woman. Tell yourself:

- With each breath, I inhale confidence, and I exhale fear. I am cool, calm and in control.
- I am flexible. I can adapt to change. I love challenges; they bring out the best in me.
- I am unique. I cherish my imperfections, and I celebrate my abilities and achievements.
- I choose inner peace over internal conflict.
- I surround myself with people who believe in me.
- I have a right to my feelings. I do not have to apologise for expressing them. I can say 'No' without feeling guilty or needing to explain my decision.
- Everyone makes mistakes. I choose to see mistakes as opportunities to learn and improve myself.

By setting goals to remove your self-destructive thought patterns and limiting beliefs gradually and by replacing these with empowering statements like the ones above, you can adopt each of the habits that confident women, French or not, use to nurture their self-worth. You can take better care of yourself, you can bring your life into balance, you can build a reliable support system, you can dramatically reduce your stress levels, you can bring yourself to forgive, and you can age as disgracefully as you want. To make it easier, you may want to try visualisation. You will find a useful Guide to Creative Visualisation at my website.

First of all, if you have not done so yet, you need to figure out exactly who you are. I would like to invite you to go back to chapter 1 and work through my suggestions. I hope you have enjoyed and have been entertained by the anecdotes in the book, but this book is not just about Anais, Inès, Lisa, Marie-Therèse, Claire, Régine, Amèlie, Corrine, Beatrice, Annie, Monique and Eloise. This book is also about YOU and how it can help YOU become supremely self-confident.

When we know who we are, we can choose who we want to become.

Conclusion

You have come to the end of this book. Yes, I know, you have not read the conclusion yet. My mission is to enable you to use your unique talents and abilities to master the skills you need to develop rock-solid self-confidence. The problem is that I cannot fit even 10% of my knowledge and experience into a book with a mere 45 000 words. Not without boring the living daylights out of you.

So you will find aids like the Vision Board guide, the Creative Visualisation guide and the Stress, Self-care, Self-Confidence and Self-Criticism Quiz that go with this book on my author website MargarethaMontagu.com.

I hope that you have found, between these pages, a confidence boosting strategy that suits you. I know that putting these principles in practice is not easy, so I use social media and my blog to continue to inspire and motivate my readers. If you have a question, do not hesitate to contact me via one of these channels:

- Blog: My blog with lots of inspirational blog posts about mindfulness, meditation and the south of France. You can subscribe to my blog at my website EquineGuidedGrowth.com

- Twitter: @EquineGuidedMD. I always let my followers know when I have published a new blog post/new book or when I am doing a giveaway. I regularly tweet stress-busting quotes, memes and tips.

- LinkedIn

- Facebook pages: Margaretha Montagu's Workshops and Books and Empower Women. I share interesting articles that I come across on the web on my Facebook page. Memes too, I love creating memes.

- Pinterest: Margaretha's Muse Here you can explore my Self-confidence, Self-compassion, Self-talk and Support Systems boards for more stress-busting articles, books, pictures, courses, etc. Most written by experts in the field.

And now also on Instagram as MiaMontagu.

My other Books

If you would like to buy and read any of my other books, you can find out more about them at my MargarethaMontagu.com website where you can buy the books directly. If you buy the books directly from my website, the full amount goes into hay for the horses, whereas if you buy from an online bookshop, I have to pay a hefty commission.

That is about it, I think. One last thing. I would appreciate it enormously if you would write a review for this book.

Legal Disclaimer

This is, in most part, a work of fiction. The contents are based on the author's personal experience and research. Despite the format, most names, characters, places, and incidents are the products of the author's imagination. To protect the privacy of the small number of real individuals, the names, and identifying details have been changed. Although every precaution has been taken to verify the accuracy of the information contained in this book, the author and publisher assume no responsibility for any errors or omissions. There are no representations or warranties, express or implied, about the completeness, accuracy, reliability, suitability or availability with respect to the information, products, services or related graphics contained in this e-book for any purpose. Any use of this information is at your own risk.

The entire content of this e-book is copyrighted. Copyright © 2016 by Margaretha de Klerk. All rights reserved. No part of this e-book may be reproduced, distributed, or transmitted in any form or by any means, including photocopying, recording, or other electronic or mechanical methods except in the case of brief quotations embodied in critical reviews and certain other non-commercial uses permitted by copyright law. For permission requests, write to the author and publisher, addressed at this e-mail address: margarethamontagu@gmail.com

This e-book is licensed for your personal enjoyment only. This e-book may not be re-sold or given away to other people. If you would like to share this book with another person, please purchase an additional copy for each recipient. If you're reading this book and did not purchase it, or it was not purchased for your use only, please return to your favourite e-book retailer and purchase your own copy. Thank you for respecting the hard work of this author.

Medical Disclaimer

All the information in this book is purely of educational value and is not intended as a substitute for proper medical care. It is not intended for use as medical therapeutic or diagnostic purposes. The resources in this book are tools for personal growth and as such are not intended for the treatment or diagnosis of any medical condition. Personal development activities present elements of emotional risk. You are responsible for your own emotional health during and after reading this book. The book is designed to accelerate your progress by providing greater focus and awareness of possibilities leading to more empowering choices. Results are due to an individual's intentions, motivation, choices and actions, supported by the material presented. The author of this book assumes no responsibility or liability for the use of the information presented in this book.

The Connect with Horses

Personal Empowerment Workshops

Based on Mindfulness and Meditation

My Twitter profile says I am a "recycled MD, a writer and mindfulness and meditation workshop presenter." In a nutshell, that is about right. You already know that I am a writer. In addition to this book, you may also have read Mindfulness and Meditation Options featuring Equine-guided Mindfulness Meditation. If not, you can read an extract at the end of this book. I also present Connect with Horses mindfulness and meditation workshops. You may have noticed a couple of not-so-subtle references to my workshops in this book. You may have wondered what it is all about, especially Equine-assisted Experiential Learning (EEL). Did I mention EEL? I am sure I did. I must have. Several times. You may even, in desperation, have clicked on an EEL link and you may now know exactly what EEL is.

The reason I mention the workshops so often is because one of the best ways to find the right meditation method for you is to try out the different methods, with guidance, until you find one that fits. That is certainly true about equine guided meditation. The best way to see if it will work for you is to try it out in person, in the presence of horses. (For those of you who love horses and who would love to spend some time in their presence but cannot do so, for whatever reason, at this moment in time, I have created the equine-guided mindfulness meditation online course (EMMOC.) You can access it at my website EquineGuidedGrowth.com) Hosting the workshops is one of my favourite activities of all times, so I would much rather show you how it works, in person.

As you have seen, each of the chapters in this book starts with an e-mail, a text or a telephone call that I received from a potential workshop participant. I couldn't very well NOT mention the workshops. If these rather too frequently-occurring references are starting to get on your nerves, I apologise. I will stop doing it immediately. I will make everything clear right away. At the end of this chapter, you will know everything you ever wanted to know about my Connect with Horses workshops.

I initially created these workshops because I am obsessed with helping people manage stress more effectively. Mindfulness and meditation can help you deal more effectively with stress. It can help you avoid the physical and mental damage that stress can cause. That is why I set out to write this book, to help people manage stress with mindfulness and meditation. It was just going to be a standard "Find the right meditation method for you" book. As you may have gathered, my horses had other ideas.

"Thanks again for sharing your life with us! I had such a wonderful time at your place and in your company. I feel revitalised, relaxed and blessed. All the best and big hugs for the two of you and all the cats, horses and dog." E.G. Meijling

"A powerful and wonderful life experience, with caring guidance. One can truly experience a mindful meditation with the horses who are definitely spiritual. Also, your senses become reinvigorated with the beautiful food and wine, whilst sitting and listening to the unique sound of nature's calmness." S. Murphy

Why would you want to attend a Connect with Horses Personal Development workshop?

Right, this chapter is supposed to be about my workshops. So, the idea of the workshops is to offer participants the chance to get away from the challenges and demands of everyday life. When you attend one of my workshops here in the south of France, you will have time to rest, to reflect and to recharge your batteries. You will be able to leave the complexity of your daily life behind, with all its demands, deadlines, doubts and disagreements. You will be encouraged to:

- put yourself first without feeling guilty,
- discover or re-discover your life's purpose,
- uncover your full potential,
- spend time "being" rather than "doing,"
- de-stress and learn how to manage stress more effectively,
- re-connect with your authentic self,

- look at your life from a distance and from a different perspective,
- eradicate limiting beliefs that hold you back,
- get rid of unhealthy habits,
- make new, like-minded friends,
- exchange your inner critic for an inner cheerleader,
- spend time enjoying the beauty of nature,
- boost your creativity,
- find inspiration and motivation to make permanent changes,
- investigate mindfulness and meditation as effective stress management strategies,
- choose the meditation technique that works best for you
- focus on what is important to you,
- forget about the shopping you need to do, the food you need to cook, the dishes you need to wash,
- experiment with leaving your comfort zone,
- say what you want to say without having to worry about the consequences,
- rebuild your shattered self-image,
- process past experiences,
- count your blessings,
- sleep peacefully and undisturbed for as long as you need to,
- stop making excuses
- and just be YOU.

A substantial number of you will read this book, I hope, will choose a meditation method that works for them and succeed in managing stress much more effectively. A small number of you will find the idea of trying out the various meditation methods while staying in one of the most beautiful parts of France irresistible. Eh bien, you are soooooo very welcome here if you feel the need to get away from all the hustle-and-bustle, not only to rest but also to be able to concentrate fully on what you want to learn. These workshops offer you the opportunity to deepen your awareness of yourself, of other people, of horses and of the world around you. My mindfulness meditation workshops are personal transformational and empowerment workshops that can be challenging and life-changing experiences.

This is where Equine-assisted Experiential Learning comes in.

The aim of my workshops is to enable women (and a few men too along the way) to put the principles described in this book into practice with the help of our horses. These personal empowerment workshops are unique because they offer participants the opportunity to discover equine-assisted experiential learning (EEL) and equine-guided mindfulness.

EEL will help you:

- free yourself from immobilising fear and so dramatically increase your self-confidence,
- discover simple techniques to easily and effectively deal with stressful situations
- communicate more efficiently and with more assertiveness,
- find out how to accept and appreciate yourself,
- strengthen and deepen relationships at work and at home,
- eradicate limiting beliefs and replace them with empowering beliefs,
- develop more successful problem-solving skills,
- thrive on change and challenges and
- gain a solid understanding of who you are now.

Having thus substantially increased your self-confidence, you could

- leave your dead-end job and find a much better one,
- ask for that raise you know you deserve,
- start the business you have always dreamed of owning,
- go back to school and get the qualifications you want,
- build solid relationships with your significant other, your parents, your children, your friends and family...

Do you feel over-burdened by the trials and tribulations of life? Do you feel physically exhausted and mentally strangled and desperately long to escape? Would you like to develop more successful problem-solving skills, communicate more effectively, build healthier relationships and significantly increase your self-confidence? If you do, then a Connect with Horses Mindfulness Meditation workshop in the sun-drenched south of France may just be exactly what you need to help you put the principles discussed in this book into practice.

If you are looking for a purely relaxing spa retreat, spending your days detoxing and being pampered, then a Connect with Horses personal empowerment workshop is not for you. If you want to relax and get away from it all, but you also want to take a good look at who you are now and where you want to go from here, then one of our workshops would be a good investment in your personal wellbeing. Our participants attend 3/5/7 or 10-day workshops. To find out more, visit EquineGuidedGrowth.com or e-mail me on at welcome2gascony@gmail.com.

Free Preview

Mindfulness and Meditation Options

Staying focused in a fast-paced World

Featuring Equine-guided Mindfulness Meditation

By Margaretha Montagu

(nom de plume de Dr Margaretha de Klerk)

MargarethaMontagu.com

EquineGuidedGrowth.com

MargarethaMontagu@gmail.com

Previously published as Mindfulness and Meditation in the south of France by SemperEquus

FOREWORD

Dear Reader

Thank you so much for buying this book, I am sure that you are going to benefit enormously from reading it. To explain why I am so sure, I need you to understand WHY I wrote this book, my longest book to date. There must be hundreds of books and e-books on the market about mindfulness and thousands about meditation. If you are interested in meditation, you have probably read several excellent books already.

So why did I write yet another book about mindfulness and meditation? It wrote this book because I want to share with you how absolutely awesome equine-guided mindfulness meditation is. Take it from me, there is nothing else quite like it. Even if you are not that keen to come face to face with a horse (because they are HUGE and might be dangerous and even deadly,) you will find this book valuable way beyond your expectations.

I only recently discovered how powerful equine-led mindfulness meditation can be. I hosted Connect with Horses personal empowerment workshops here in the south of France, based on equine-assisted personal development for the past 10 years. I have long known what a tremendous difference it can make to my clients' lives. In the last three years, I added equine-guided meditation to the mixture, so meditating in the presence of horses is not entirely new to me. In the equine-guided meditation chapter in this book, you can read about how I "accidentally" discovered this practice. It was only in the last 18 months though, that I discovered how much it could help me, personally.

In the last 18 months, due to my ongoing eye problems, I have not been able to ride much. I am seriously into classical riding, or dressage, as it is also known. I have been obsessed with studying this riding discipline for the last ten years. Not being able to ride regularly, as I had to have one eye operation after another, was mind-numbing. I had to find something else to do with my horses. I had to find a different way to be with my horses. I fell deeper into equine-guided meditation, once again, more or less by accident, rather than by design. My eye surgeon advised me not to do anything that could precipitate another retinal detachment. As far as I could gather, that meant that all I could do with the horses was be with them, without actually doing anything.

If you know me, you will understand how crippling not being able to do anything is to me.

I already knew that just being in the presence of horses can be an exercise in mindfulness meditation. Now I discovered that watching them graze through the window on the days that I could not go outside could work as well as a mindfulness meditation exercise. I discovered that in the long and often painful hours of the night, that looking at pictures of my horses is as effective as seeing them in real life. Same goes for looking at video of horses grazing peacefully. My ultimate discovery was that I could mindfully meditate, just by imagining being with my horses. I have read, when

I studied visualisation, that our minds cannot distinguish between what we imagine is happening and what is really happening. You can read more about this method of meditation in the "Visualisation Meditation" chapter of this book.

While in hospital, I tried imagining that I am actually with the horses, making it as real as I possibly could by using all five my senses (down to the aroma and taste of the first cup of coffee of the morning that I usually have while I watch them through the kitchen window.) I found that this sort of visualisation meditation is as powerful - maybe even more so! - than had I been within touching distance of m horses. If you have read some of my other books you may know that I highly recommend journaling, even if you start small by keeping a bullet-point gratitude diary. As is my custom, I kept a diary of my experiences and in this latest edition of this book, I share with you what I have learned: about myself, about mindfulness meditation and about the mind-blowing soothing and healing ability of horses.

As I got better, I added some of my other favourite meditation methods to the equine-guided model. Walking meditation became mindfully walking and meditating with horses. Working meditation became grooming horses mindfully while meditating. Music meditation became listening to music with the horses and noting the effect it has on them, especially drumming. Writing meditation became making an equine-inspired gratitude list. Etc.

This book, which I wrote originally as an accompanying workbook to our workshops, is now about sharing my discoveries with not only our workshop participants but with everyone who has ever felt drawn to horses and is interested in mindful meditation. When you have read this book, you will not only know a lot more about mindfulness but also a good deal about 12 different meditation methods, including equine-guided mindfulness meditation.

It is my dearest wish that this book will make a difference in your life, for the better and in the long-term. The ultimate intent of this book is not only to introduce you to equine-guided mindfulness meditation, but also equip you with a toolbox full of tools that will help cope with life's challenges as well as enable you to live a life full of purpose and meaning.

By the way, all the downloads mentioned in the e-book version of this book are free and that the book contains NO affiliate links. Also, I would also hugely appreciate it if you would let me know if you find spelling mistakes in the text. English is not my first language, so despite my best intentions, mistakes do slip in.

All the best,

Margaretha

PS. Have you subscribed to my blog's mailing list yet? If you have already subscribed, thank you so much! If not, please do. It will enable me to continue to support you in your quest to become your best self, once you have finished reading this book. The aim of my blog is to assist you to make the most of yourself and to provide you with the tools to do so. The blog has a distinctly French flavour, as I also share with you our life here in the south of France. You can subscribe at my website EquineGuidedGrowth.com. Just fill in your e-mail address to receive news of my workshops here in the south of France with details of last-minute discounts and early bird special offers, available only to my mailing list subscribers. Your e-mail address is 100% safe and you can unsubscribe from my blog at any time.

☐

INTRODUCTION

Have you ever wondered: (I know I have!)

Why do I attract so many challenging situations?

Why do I feel so tired all the time and why do I have no energy to accomplish anything?

This book can help you to re-condition your mind using mindfulness and meditation to stop attracting challenging events, situations and relationships into your life and instead attract success, energy, prosperity and abundance into your life. In this book, I introduce you to the tools I use during my personal empowerment workshops: equine-assisted experiential learning and a variety of mindfulness meditation methods, including equine-guided mindfulness meditation.

Mindfulness

• enables you to deal with distractions more effectively so that you can concentrate easily and increase your productivity both at home and at work

• makes you more creative and so that you can solve problems faster as it helps you to let go of doubts that might otherwise block your creativity

• helps you to sleep better at night so that you are not tired all the time and can get a lot more done during the day.

• enhances your mental agility and alertness, increases cognitive recall and protects you from memory loss as you get older

• gives you time to think before you act, making it easier to control your anger and listen more effectively so that you get on better with family, friends and colleagues

• dramatically lowers your stress levels so that you can cope effectively with the challenges that come your way. It also makes you physically and mentally healthier and more resilient while helping you avoid the damage stress can do to our minds and bodies

• makes you more compassionate towards others and towards yourself so that you can accept yourself, forgive yourself and love yourself just as you are

As with my book Self-Confidence Made Simple, I have also made a Playlist for this book. It is called Equine Enchantment and you can watch it or listen to it on my YouTube channel (Margaretha Montagu), while you continue reading. The first video is about Andrea Bocelli, the blind opera singer. In the video, Andrea rides a beautiful dressage stallion, Sir César. For me, already blind in one eye and with ongoing problems in the other, this video has been immensely inspiring. Apart from having its own playlist, Mindfulness and Meditation Options differs from other books about mindfulness and meditation in five unique ways:

1. This book is not just a collection of explanations and instructions. It is a book full of suggestions and solutions. I wrote this book because I passionately believe in the transformational power of mindfulness meditation, especially guided by horses. I believe that mindfulness and meditation are highly effective stress management strategies that can help practitioners avoid the physical and mental damage that stress can cause. That is why it is of primordial importance to me to help you find a meditation method that suits you, whether it is equine-guided on not. A method that you will be able to incorporate into your daily life without having to sacrifice too much of your precious time. A method that you will be able to continue practising daily, for the rest of your life.

2. This book proposes a technique, in the form of a questionnaire, to help you choose the meditation method will work the best for you. Meditation is not a one-size-fits-all exercise. We are all different, we each have to find a meditation method that suits us, mentally and physically.

3. This book helps readers solve real-life problems. In each chapter, an everyday person with everyday challenges explains his/her problem. There is

- someone who struggles to lose weight and keep it off,
- someone with relationship problems,
- someone who cannot sleep,
- someone with an overwhelmingly stressful job,
- someone whose new business is faltering,
- someone who is trying to make a long-treasured dream come true,
- someone who wants to grow spiritually...

The rest of each chapter demonstrates how each of these people can solve their problem with mindfulness and meditation.

4. This book contains a chapter explaining what equine-guided mindfulness meditation is and how to practise it.

5. This book (the e-book version) is an interactive and practical aid – each chapter contains a selection of links to further resources, carefully chosen to help the reader discover and experience the

various meditation methods presented. There are also links to scientific studies that back up the effectiveness of the methods described in the book.

Mindfulness and Meditation Options aims answer your questions about mindfulness and meditation and especially about equine-guided mindfulness meditation. In this book, I also investigate the scientific studies that have been conducted about both mindfulness and meditation. I will introduce you to a variety of different meditation methods:

- walking meditation,
- working meditation,
- writing meditation,
- music meditation,
- visualisation meditation,
- contemplative meditation,
- equine-guided meditation and gratitude meditation
- sleep meditation
- as well as breathing meditation.

Each chapter starts with a letter written to me by a potential participant in one of the personal empowerment workshops we host here in the south of France. Each letter reveals a specific problem, or set of problems that readers will be able to identify with. The letter is followed by a detailed explanation of how to solve the writer's problems using mindfulness and meditation. If you too would like to find out more about mindfulness and meditation and how it can benefit you in a practical and sustainable way, this is the book for you.

CHAPTER 1

WHAT IS MEDITATION?

"The soul always knows what to do to heal itself. The challenge is to silence the mind."

Caroline Myss

Meditate, moi? I didn't think so.

I used to be sceptic about meditation. I had a vague notion of what meditation is and that people meditate to relax. Being as obsessed with stress management as I am, that did sound marginally interesting. It is just that sitting still for hours on end did not appeal to me at all. Honestly, I had way too much to do to waste time sitting around doing nothing the whole day long. There aren't enough hours in the day as it is.

I did notice, as I suspect all horse owners and many horse riders do, that when I spend time with my horses, just being with them, I tend to end up in a more peaceful place spiritually. I also discovered that when I am with one or more of my horses, being mindful is easier, nearly effortless. There is enormous comfort to be had, on a cold winter's morning, from taking my soul mare Belle into the barn and grooming her unhurriedly, gently easing away the knots in her muscles and basking in her unconditional love and quiet understanding, far from the worries and troubles of my average day.

It was only, when a meditating friend said to me, "You know, you already meditate, without even realising, for long periods every day, when you are with your horses. I have seen you at it many times," that I sat up and took notice. Meditate, moi?

I didn't think so.

"Oh yes," she said, "when you are grooming the horses, you become so focused on what you are doing, that everything else fades into non-existence." At the time, I fervently denied it, insisting that grooming is more like self-hypnosis, nothing to do with meditation. When this very good friend of mine piped up: "You haven't got a clue what meditation is, do you?" I ignored her and continued grooming the Duke, who by that time was melting into a pool of utter bliss.

Her words did make me think, though.

Fine. What IS meditation? I thought I had better look it up as I am supposed to be this highly-qualified stress management expert.

More and more of my contemporaries were suggesting that meditation may well be a very effective antidote to the damage stress can do to sufferers' mental and physical health. According to Merriam-Webster, mediation is about "spending time in quiet thought for religious purposes or for relaxation," and to meditate is to "engage in contemplation or reflection" and "to engage in mental exercise (as concentration on one's breathing or repetition of a mantra) for the purpose of reaching a heightened level of spiritual awareness." Well, all those big words weren't particularly helpful.

Wikipedia was a bit more useful: "Meditation is a practice in which an individual train the mind or induces a mode of consciousness, either to realise some benefit or for the mind to simply acknowledge its content without becoming identified with that content." Right, but how would that benefit the person who is doing the meditation? How will it work for me, here on the farm, looking after the horses? How will it benefit people with sky-high stress-levels?

In this chapter, to help us understand what meditation is, we are going to look at

1. The definition of Meditation
2. The benefits of Meditation

You may have bought this book because you are interested in meditation as a stress management technique. For you, I have included a Stress Quiz at the end of this chapter. The quiz will help you find out how stress you are right at this moment. Once you have established a meditation practice, you can take the quiz again and use it to measure the effectiveness of meditation as a stress management method.

END OF PREVIEW

This book will introduce you to the tools, mindfulness and meditation, with or without horses, that you need to completely transform your life into exactly what you want it to be. You can buy it, as well as my other books, at my website

MargarethaMontagu.com or at most online bookshops. You can buy this book directly from my website. As I mentioned, if you buy the books directly from my website, the full amount goes into hay for the horses, whereas if you buy from an online bookshop, I have to pay a hefty commission.

Le succès est souvent atteint par ceux qui ne savent pas que l'échec est inévitable.

Coco Chanel

Bibliography

The Bible

The Success Principles, Life Lessons for mastering the Law of Attraction, The power of Focus, Chicken Soup for the Soul by Jack Canfield

Feel the Fear and Beyond, End the Struggle and Dance With Life, Embracing Uncertainty, The Feel the Fear Guide to Lasting Love, Life is Huge! by Susan Jeffers

Finding your own North Star, Steering by Starlight by Martha Beck

The 7 Habits of Highly Effective People, First Things First by Stephen R. Covey.

The Miracle of Tithing by Mark Victor Hansen.

Awaken The Giant, Unlimited Power by Anthony Robbins.

Boundaries: When to Say Yes, When to Say No to Take Control of Your Life by Dr. Henry Cloud and Dr. John Townsend.

The Power of Now: A Guide to Spiritual Enlightenment by Eckhart Tolle.

The Aladdin Factor: How to Ask for and Get What You Want in Every Area of Your Life by Jack Canfield and Mark Victor Hansen.

The Six Pillars of Self-Esteem: The Definitive Work on Self-Esteem Nathaniel Branden

The Gifts of Imperfection: Let Go of Who You Think You're Supposed to Be and Embrace Who You Are by Brené Brown, Ph.D., L.M.S.W.

The Obstacle is the Way: The Timeless Art of Turning Trials into Triumph by Ryan Holiday

The Purpose Driven Life by Rick Warren

Man's Search for Meaning by Victor Frankl

Being Happy! by Andrew Matthews

Manifest Your Destiny: The Nine Spiritual Principles for Getting Everything You Want by Wayne W. Dyer.

Creative Visualisation by Shakti Gawain.

The Power of Positive Thinking by Norman Vincent Peale

The Alchemist: A Fable About Following Your Dream by Paulo Coelho

Wherever you go, There you are by Jon Kabat-Zinn

The Magic of Thinking Big by David J. Schwartz

How to make Friends and influence People, How to Stop Worrying and Start Living by Dale Carnegie

A Return to Love: Reflections on the Principles of A Course in Miracles, A Woman' Worth, The Gift of Change by Marianne Williamson

The Road less Travelled by Scott Peck

You can heal your Life by Louise Hay

The Simple Abundance Journal of Gratitude by Sarah Ban Breathnach

Horse Sense and the Human Heart - What Horses Can Teach Us About Trust, Bonding, Creativity and Spirituality by Adele von Rust McCormick and Marlena Deborah McCormick

More recommendations at MargarethaMontagu.com

Printed in Great Britain
by Amazon